CRISIS IN THE PRIMARY CLASSROOM

Maurice Galton

David Fulton Publishers

London

David Fulton Publishers Ltd
2 Barbon Close, London WC1N 3JX

First published in Great Britain by
David Fulton Publishers 1995

Note: The right of Maurice Galton to be identified as the author of this work has been
asserted by him in accordance with the Copyright, Designs and Patents Act 1988.

Copyright © Maurice Galton

British Library Cataloguing in Publication Data

A catalogue record for this book is available from the British Library

ISBN 1-85346-245-4

Typeset by RP Typesetters Ltd., Unit 13, 21 Wren Street, London WC1X 0HF.

Printed in Great Britain by BPC Books & Journals, Exeter.

Contents

List of Tables

Personal Prologue

This was a book I did not expect to write. In 1988, when the National Curriculum was introduced as part of the Education Reform Act, I was invited to join a lobby group set up to fight for the survival of comprehensive education. The founder members of the group believed that sections of the Act undermined the principles of the comprehensive system and that the new curriculum proposals would bring about the return of a rigid and traditional subject-dominated timetable. This would make life more difficult for teachers already struggling to motivate sizeable numbers of disaffected pupils.

At the time, I refused to become a member. I argued that to engage in a debate of this kind, before the evidence had emerged, would reinforce the views of Right-wing groups, such as the Centre for Policy Studies, that the LEAs and university education departments would deliberately set out to undermine government policy. We should then be blamed collectively for any failures. Such accusations were already being made by government education ministers. One of them, attending a meeting of the University Council for the Education of Teachers (UCET) had demanded and been given assurances by Professor Ted Wragg, a regular critic of government policy through his satirical column in *The Times Educational Supplement*, that as loyal citizens, teacher trainers were committed to do their best to implement policies which the electorate had voted upon and endorsed.

In my letter of refusal I also argued that there were grounds for taking the optimistic view that the government would eventually 'tone down' some of its proposals. This view was informed by what curriculum theory, particularly that concerning the implementation of change in schools, had to say about 'top-down models' of innovation. I also could not see how the National Curriculum could succeed without a healthy layer of middle management, such as that provided by LEAs, to act as a bridge between policy makers and those attempting to implement policy at classroom level. This view was reinforced by my experience as a consultant for the Council of Europe's Primary Project during the mid-1980s. The trends noted in the Project group's report had led those continental member states of the Council for Cultural

Cooperation, the Council of Europe (CDCC), with centralized education systems, to transfer more powers to the local regions.

However, my main reason for not joining the lobby group was a personal one. Throughout the 1980s, a series of classroom studies on primary schools had more or less reached a consensus about the problems facing teachers in providing young children with a 'sound start' and in preparing them for transfer to secondary schools. It was fairly well established that there had been no 'golden age' either before or after the setting up of the Plowden Committee and that, in particular, Plowden had not given rise to a 'primary revolution' based upon extreme progressive views. The central problem was that teachers had continued to use the same tactics when engaging with pupils but that the change to mixed ability groups now required the balance in classroom organization to shift in favour of individualization. The combination of these old tactics and the new organizational strategy was proving not only stressful, because of the effort it required of teachers, but also unproductive in the use of pupils' time. The major need, therefore, was to create an effective system of professional development, including the element of initial teacher training, which would no longer sustain existing practice.

In the United States, and indeed all over the world, the same debate was taking place. In 1991, therefore, I was given a travelling Fellowship by The Leverhulme Trust to visit America and other countries to look at training systems. I wished to develop models of professional development which would create in teachers an expectation of moving through clearly defined stages. At the same time, the University of Leicester was engaged in a large research programme using principles of action planning to chart the progress of its PGCE students. The novice teacher's action plan was to become the basis for a Record of Achievement which could then be passed onto schools to help plan induction programmes. Capitalizing on our existing knowledge of primary classrooms and developing new models of professional development therefore seemed to be the crucial item on the research agenda for the 1990s. Rather than renewing the old battles between progressive and traditional teaching approaches as part of the lobby group, I preferred to give my time to these more important issues.

Clearly, events have proved me wrong and the founder members of this lobby group correct. In 1988 I had agreed to join the National Curriculum Interim Primary Committee with the idea that some of these emerging pedagogic issues might be sketched out in our report. In the event, I was to find that ownership of the report was taken away from the committee members and the final version produced so that it contained only evidence which reinforced the government's own agenda. With the coming and going of various education ministers the situation has become more extreme. I found my own work quoted in ministerial documents, or rather misquoted, to support the prejudices being expressed. When Robin Alexander asked for my views on behalf of his three-man committee, I wrote back, citing my own experiences of the National Curriculum Council. I told him that I doubted whether he would be free to produce the kind of report he wanted despite the assurances he had received.

In the event this time I was to be proved right. What I did not foresee however was the new alliance between the 'Right' and the new 'middle-class' Left (referred to by some as the 'futon socialists'). At various times, in recent years, both main political parties have called for the reintroduction of streaming at the top end of the junior school. After the publication of the so-called 'Three Wise Men's' report, the quality press, with the exception of *The Independent*, repeatedly criticized Professor Alexander for his attempt to move the debate away from crude denunciations of existing primary practice. *The Guardian*, which throughout the debate in the 1970s and 1980s adopted a balanced view, took a particularly hard line. The paper's editorial singled out for praise the comments of another member of the three-man team who criticized some primary teachers in language reminiscent of the Black Paper writers of the late 1970s.

Perhaps my own involvement with the press at the time was not atypical. One day I was phoned by a reporter from *The Mail on Sunday* and invited to meet her in London to discuss my work. I was assured that ministers were interested in issues of teaching and that this reporter felt my ideas would be of value. The lady in question assured me that her motives were sound, adding by way of evidence in support of her good intentions that her boyfriend worked for Brent council! During the course of tea I therefore offered her my views. Notwithstanding this discussion, when I bought *The Mail on Sunday* the headline read, 'Professor says, "Place pupils back in rows"'. The article was syndicated to local weekly papers and for some months I received angry letters from teachers accusing me of betraying their trust. This had little to do with the reporter who allowed me to alter her copy before submission; I was told to blame the sub-editor for the selective cuts.

These experiences led me to believe that it was no longer possible, nor defensible, to remain outside the debate, particularly because, recently, any pretence at using existing research evidence to justify policy has been abandoned. Instead, unsubstantiated prejudices and hearsay have been used to support further change. One despairs at times that so many of these current myths about primary teachers are accepted by education writers and broadcasters in the quality media. One suspects that these people, while happy at their Hampstead and Islington dinner parties to parade egalitarian views are, at the same time, seeking excuses for taking their own children out of the state system. At present, therefore, with no political 'mileage' to be gained by standing up for primary education, there is a danger of even greater collapse of teacher morale and a fatalistic acceptance of the status quo. This danger has been exacerbated by the fact that the National Curriculum, by judging the 'fitness for purpose' (a favourite HMI term) of classroom tasks by the number of attainment targets covered, rather than their capacity to meet the children's learning needs, has tended to reduce teaching to a mere technical activity.

Yet there are some hopeful signs that many teachers are still resisting this diminution of their professionalism. A year ago I gave the keynote presentation at a well-attended meeting of primary headteachers in East Anglia. What should have been an hour's presentation turned into a whole day's discussion about issues concerning teaching and learning. The general sentiment expressed by the audience was that they were now coping with the demands of the National Curriculum and what they couldn't cope with they were no longer prepared to bother with. What these headteachers wanted was to concentrate on the schools' central mission. This sought to develop in children an intellectual curiosity which would sustain them for life, despite the sometimes mundane experiences they would receive during their secondary education. At the same time, primary schools also had to provide pupils with the basic tools which would compensate them for the inequalities elsewhere in the system and would equip them for whatever lay ahead in the twenty-first century. These are not easy tasks. I hope that this book can make a small contribution to the debate about the means to achieve these end.

Finally, some thanks are due. First, to friends and colleagues for helpful discussions. Second, to my family for their patience and toler-ance. Last, but not least, to Dianne Stroud, who has worked with me since the ORACLE project. Her efficiency, good humour and careful attention to detail has made it possible to complete this book without too much personal pain.

Chapter 1
The Primary Education Debate

New Record but Same Old Tune

In the last few years it has become fairly commonplace to find government papers on education making references to, and in some cases actually quoting, research findings on primary teaching, although many of these references refer to work which was carried out in the 1970s or early 1980s. Whatever the reasons for this time-lag, the research is now used to justify demands for more class teaching, increased streaming within classes through the use of ability groups, severe restrictions on the use of topic work and more single-subject teaching in junior age classes.

There are those who see these policy changes as a consequence of the application of a 'market forces' approach to the public sector by recent governments. Yet criticism of what is generally termed 'modern primary practice' has a much longer history. It goes back to the debates in the 1930s, through the post-war years, before moving to a peak which coincided with the abolition of streaming and the introduction of comprehensive education in the late 1960s and early 1970s. From these criticisms arose the so-called 'Great Debate', instituted by the then Prime Minister, James Callaghan, leading eventually to the 1988 Education Reform Act and the establishment of a National Curriculum. What can be said of this later period, even before teachers withdrew their cooperation over testing, is that the debate had become more strident and polarized.

This most recent round of debate, and the consequent changes it has generated, has produced a crisis of confidence among many primary teachers, manifested by a loss of direction and focus. It is argued by some that this is a temporary state and that once the initial difficulties encountered with the delivery of the National Curriculum and the corresponding assessments have been mastered, teachers will once more begin to extend their horizons as confidence returns. For those who think in this way it is the pace of change rather than the change itself which is the problem. Others, however, argue that the problem stems from the way in which the National Curriculum and the related testing programme has been imposed upon the profession, reducing the scope for decision making in the classroom to a point where teachers have become technicians rather than skilled managers of a complex learning environment.

This book explores both propositions. It examines the question of how far there are fundamental flaws in the methods we use to teach young children and whether the advice now being offered is adequate and, more importantly, correct. In doing so it will look at the assumptions that lie behind the advice now being offered to teachers, particularly that based upon the argument that certain beliefs about how children learn have had too great an influence on the way in which teachers teach, This view has led policy makers to conclude that, if the part played by Local Education Authorities and universities in training teachers is reduced, schools will return to well tried traditional practices.

Before engaging on this exploration, however, it is necessary to do two things. First, to provide a brief historical overview of developments in primary education during the period since the second world war in order to set the present debate in a proper context. Second, to look at some of the factors which influence, constrain and eventually determine the ways in which curriculum aims are translated into practice, for it is one thing to produce a curriculum blueprint on paper but another to ensure the implementation of that blueprint in a wide variety of school contexts.

Change and Continuity in the Primary School

It is not generally appreciated by those who complain about the current changes now taking place in primary education that there is very little new in this situation. As Brian Simon reminds us (Galton *et al.*, 1980) it was only in 1928 that separate primary schools were first accepted as official policy and only in the mid-1960s were all children between the ages of 5 and 11 educated in separate primary schools. This reorganization had barely been completed before middle schools were established. Their growth in popularity coincided with the abolition of selection at age 11 and the introduction of comprehensive education. Within the further reorganization which took place, the choice of age at which children transferred from primary to middle school was more often dictated by the need to minimize the costs of these changes by using existing buildings without further modification. By the mid-1970s children somewhere in Britain faced the possibility of either transferring at age 7 from separate infant schools to a junior school or from a first school to a middle school at age 8, 9 or 10.

Although government policy set 8 as the most suitable transfer age, this recommendation was not widely taken up. Most local authorities retained their existing systems, whether they were ages 8 to 12, 9 to 13, or 10 to 14 middle schools, with each authority seeking to justify its preference by setting up working parties to derive a curriculum appropriate for the chosen age range (Hargreaves, 1980). These systems had barely been established before further changes were imposed following the attention given by the 1978 Warnock Report on the needs of children with special learning difficulties. The decline in the age cohort during the 1980s led to the inclusion of increasing numbers of the rising 5s into the first school. This latter period also saw calls for more science in the curriculum and the introduction of new subjects such as technology and computing. As the fall in population worked its way into the secondary schools, doubts were increasingly expressed about the viability of the middle school, given the rapid growth of the 16–19 sector incorporating both sixth form colleges and further education establishments.

The decline of our traditional industrial base during the 1980s and again, more recently, has also seen a decline in the quality of life within the great centres of population and a move by an increasing number of families, well educated and well off, to the outer suburbs and the rural villages surrounding our cities. Recent changes, as the result of the 1988 Education Act which enshrined the principle of parental choice of school and ensured that the funding followed pupils, has exacerbated differences between inner-city schools and those in more prosperous areas. As the ability of LEAs to support city schools with special difficulties has declined, many have had to look carefully at staffing levels and, in some cases, release experienced teachers in order to appoint cheaper probationers. In recent years, the annual reports of Her Majesty's Inspectors have pointed to a sharp decline in the infrastructure of the school system. As a result of all these changes, headteachers now find their role has rapidly changed, with increasing amounts of time being spent on administrative and financial matters to the detriment of the curriculum (Mortimore and Mortimore, 1991).

But the debate about primary education has not only concentrated on matters of organization and finance. Throughout the period a central issue has concerned the perceived benefits or defects of what is usually called 'progressive' child-centred approaches. These first came to the ascendant in the 1930s and were strongly promoted by what we would now term lobbying groups such as the Froebelian movement. However, as Simon (1993) observes, the rather primitive conditions which existed in most classrooms prevented these ideas from gaining hold in most state schools. Instead it was left to the private middle-class schools, such as those run by Susan Isaacs and by A. S. Neil at Summerhill, to implement the new philosophy. Indeed, one of the major problems in our mixed system is that the private sector is freer to adopt innovation and has often modified these new curriculum initiatives in ways which made them unsuitable for use in state schools, where cultural and social diversity produces special problems. Over the years, with the development of a multi-cultural society, this cultural diversity has increased, giving rise to complex contrasting value systems within which the school and its teachers must try to operate. I have argued elsewhere (Galton, 1989) that these cultural differences have contributed to the general public misunderstanding concerning child-centred progressive methods, with a tendency for issues to become polarized in over-simplistic terms.

When considering how to control pupil misbehaviour, for example, politicians and the media have recently argued that those in positions of authority, such as teachers, 'should condemn more and understand less'. This suggests that the only choice lies between either 'telling pupils firmly what to do' (the traditional view) or 'letting them get away with it to the extent of tolerating anarchy' (the perceived progressive option). This view of progressivism stems, in part, from a reading of accounts such as that of A.S. Neil who cured one of his pupils of thieving by repeatedly replacing the stolen coins until the pupil, either through boredom or puzzlement, eventually entered into a constructive dialogue with Neil about his problem. To see how unattractive it would be for a typical primary teacher to adopt Neil's strategy, it is only necessary to translate the same incident into a state primary school classroom on a Monday morning where a child announces to the harassed teacher, 'Miss, somebody has taken my dinner money'. Yet the persistent belief remains that primary teachers condone unpleasant behaviour as instanced by the advice to teachers in a newspaper headline in 1980: 'Stop being kind to the children'.

Teaching Styles in the Primary Classroom

The same media treatment has applied to the introduction of new teaching approaches where practices criticized were more likely to exist in some private rather state schools. Despite the Hadow Report (1931), the pressures resulting from the 11-plus, which gave rise to so much anxiety among teachers, in case their pupils had not done as well in the race for grammar school places as colleagues in the next school down the road, has meant that teachers continued to emphasize memorization through rote learning. A large proportion of time was spent on the 'Three Rs' which, along with the general intelligence test, were the major determinants of successful entry into grammar school.

During this time, the pioneering work of Dorothy Gardner attempted to show that pupils taught by less didactic methods produced as good if not better results than these more traditional approaches. These studies, however, have been criticized, notably by Anthony (1982) because they were biased in favour of child-centred approaches. One of the criteria that Gardner used to distinguish progressive classes from traditional ones was that children in the former demonstrated interest in their work. Anthony argued that Gardner in this way selected only the most effective progressive classrooms but compared these with a range of traditional classes, since the criteria used to select the latter did not consider how the children behaved but how they were organized. Like was not therefore being compared with like.

By the mid-1960s, however, little pockets of innovation had developed in various parts of the country, promoted by Chief Education Officers who were persuaded of the value of these new teaching approaches and campaigned actively for their wider use. Stewart Mason was a case in point. As recounted by Jones (1988), Mason brought in special advisers who encouraged teachers to change their practice. Elsewhere in the West Riding, under Sir Alex Clegg, similar experiments were taking place. These developments came to fruition when the evidence collected for the Newsom Report (1963), *Half Our Future*, exposed the extent to which young adults from working-class backgrounds, although possessing suitable IQ scores, had nevertheless failed to gain entry into the grammar schools stream at age 11. The growing consensus within both major political parties that such problems could only be solved by ending selection at 11 and developing a comprehensive system of secondary schooling, coincided with the setting up of a committee to report on primary education.

It has been argued by Jones (1987) that this Plowden Report (1967) and the structural changes associated with the abolition of streaming within the primary school, helped to create an impression that change in school was more radical than really it was. In particular, the use of the term, 'primary school revolution, by an American, Joseph Featherstone (1971), in a book, *Schools Where Children Learn,* not only helped to create an explosion of interest in English education among Americans, leading to the setting up of vacation workshops in the United States on which many Leicestershire teachers and colleagues from the West

Riding worked, but it also fed back into the language used to described the structural changes taking place in English schools. It is unclear whether this was where the term, 'the primary revolution' first manifested itself, but it was given credence by the existence of the much-publicized case of the William Tyndale School (Auld, 1976).

Over a quarter of a century later it is now agreed by most serious commentators that if by revolution is meant the wholehearted adoption of the Plowden recommendations, then such a revolution never took place. Simon's very careful analysis of the data collected for the Plowden Report by Her Majesty's Inspectorate concludes that less than 10 per cent met most of the criteria (Simon, 1981a). However, much damage to the reputation of primary schooling ensued, in part fed by the findings of a survey by the National Foundation for Educational Research that reading standards had fallen, a conclusion that then had to be hastily re-evaluated when further analysis of data showed that there was a flaw in the statistical method used to compare the results from different schools. The debate was further fuelled by the publication of the 'Black Paper' series, edited by two academics. It is part of the fascination of the present debate that one of these editors, Professor Brian Cox, should now be seen to be on the other side in the controversy over the teaching of English in the National Curriculum. Many of the leading Black Paper writers had no experience of state education other than at university. These critics placed the highest value on teaching individual subjects, arguing that each had its own intrinsic merit. Strong objections were raised to developments such as the integrated day, which attempted to link subjects by using topic or thematic approaches, although as Simon (1981a) demonstrates, surveys of classroom organization and practice carried out at that time showed that only a limited amount of work was organized in this way and when such work was attempted it rarely involved core subjects such as English or mathematics.

Nevertheless, educational debates of this kind are often a boon to researchers because they provide a rationale against which applications for funding can be made. The results of one such study seeking to resolve some of the questions generated by the Black Papers appeared in a book under the title, *Teaching Styles and Pupil Progress* (Bennett, 1976). Although at the time the results received widespread criticism by many within the British research community, they were endorsed by the famous American psychologist, Jerome Bruner, and taken up by the media and by the public. The first edition sold out within a few days of the BBC 'Horizon' programme which summarized the findings. These showed that pupils taught by traditional approaches appeared to improve their scores on language, reading and computation compared to those taught by progressive teachers. The results produced considerable controversy and over the next few years the arguments tended to become more obscure, so much so that by 1981 Bennett was keen to argue that his description of teachers as either *formal* or *informal* and *traditional* or *progressive* had 'perhaps now outlived their usefulness' (*Times Educational Supplement*, 24 July 1981).

Looking back on this era, however, it is now possible to conclude that, whatever the weakness in the methods of analysis, the main findings of Bennett's studies have been frequently replicated both in the United Kingdom and in the United States. Where teaching effectiveness is defined solely in terms of pupil performance on standardized tests of mathematics and language, moderate positive correlations have been found between these measures and the extent to which pupils were taught as a whole class as opposed to being provided with individual assignments (Brophy and Good, 1986).

One result of this public interest in primary education was the inauguration of 'The Great Debate' by the then Prime Minister, James (now Lord) Callaghan, in his Ruskin speech of October 1976. There he voiced concern about the basic teaching of the three Rs, the relevance of the curriculum, particularly in science and mathematics, the adequacy of the present examination system and the need for a reform of education for 16–19-year-olds. Among other concerns raised in the speech was 'the unease felt by parents and others about new informal methods of teaching which seem to produce excellent results when they are in well qualified hands but are much more dubious when they are not' (Callaghan, 1976).

Writing some 16 years later, Lord Callaghan complains that all too soon the issues raised in 1976 were removed from the agenda while others took their place. The result is that since that time the debate about teaching methods has made little progress (Callaghan, 1992). Lord Callaghan endorses the conclusion of Sir Claus Moser's presidential address to the British Association for the Advancement of Science, that 'this country is now in danger of becoming one of the least adequately educated of all advanced nations' (Moser, 1990) and suggests this is a despairing verdict on the past and a horrific forecast for the future. Against such pessimistic prognosis there has been a torrent of legislation with 'so much change in methods, contents and structures that teachers complain of innovation fatigue' (Callaghan, 1992, p.10). Lord Callaghan concludes by endorsing Moser's call for 'a leap forward in the quality and vision of the educational goals we set ourselves'.

Classroom Processes and Pupil Behaviour

The question of why, given the evidence which emerged towards the end of the 1970s, little systematic change took place in the ways that schools organized teaching and learning, will be explored at several points throughout this book as the argument develops. Returning to Bennett's (1976) research and the claims that class teaching was a more effective means of ensuring pupil progress in the core skills of numeracy and literacy, there was little in that research which explained what it was that teachers who taught in this way did that enabled such progress to be achieved. The ORACLE (Observational Research and Classroom Learning Evaluation) studies carried out at the University of Leicester over the period 1975–83 (Galton, 1987) attempted to answer such questions by, as the name of the project suggests, directly observing teachers and pupils during lessons, in some cases over a three-year period.

The conclusions of these studies were that it was not in itself class teaching or individualized instruction which made the difference but the opportunity that the use of a particular method provided for a teacher to engage in certain types of exchanges with pupils. When class teaching was used, for example, there was a greater probability that teachers would ask more challenging questions of their pupils and that pupils would pay more attention and concentrate more on their work. Consequently, there would be fewer disruptions which distracted both teachers and other pupils from the tasks in hand. Another advantage which this style of teaching seemed to enjoy was that it enabled teachers to provide greater amounts of feedback to pupils about the quality of their work.

There were, of course, disadvantages in this whole-class approach in that a sizeable number of pupils remained largely inactive during these exchanges, preferring to listen to the teacher either when she or he addressed the whole class or was questioning individuals or groups of pupils. The point that needs to be stressed when considering these results, however, is that none of these kinds of exchanges between pupils and teachers is an unique attribute of class teaching. It is possible to visualize a teacher, with pupils who are working on different individual assignments, engaging in the same kinds of exchanges (or interactions). Indeed, in the ORACLE sample, a small group of teachers who worked in this way, did succeed in matching teachers who mainly used a whole-class approach in their use of these interactions. These teachers worked at a very demanding pace, engaging in conversations with individual pupils for nearly 90 per cent of the day compared to an average of 75 per cent in the rest of the sample. When the test results of pupils in the classes of this extremely active group of teachers were analysed, it was found that they compared very favourably with those of the pupils who experienced greater amounts of whole-class teaching.

Thus it was not class teaching in itself which brought about success but what could be accomplished when teachers taught in this way. The bulk of teachers, who preferred approaches based on individual assignments, were unable to match these class teachers in the use of certain types of interaction, such as asking challenging questions or providing feedback. In many of the classrooms where setting individual assignments was the teacher's preference, there were more disruptions with the result that children spent considerably less time on task.

These lower levels of interaction did not arise because the teachers were any less capable when employing questioning techniques. It was rather that their preferred organizational strategy – setting individual assignments – denied them opportunities to use these teaching skills, largely, it would appear, because of the over-dependence of children on the teacher as a source of information. Children would be reluctant to risk offering answers to a problem until they had either consulted the teacher for guidance or spent time listening to the teacher talking to another pupil, in the hope that the exchange provided a clue as to the solution of their own problem. Because of this dependency, teachers were forced to spend more and more of their time ensuring that children were able to continue on their tasks. Thus there were above average levels (compared to the rest of the sample) of exchanges where teacher either provided children with instructions about what to do next or provided information which was needed to complete a task.

In such classes there were often queues of pupils waiting for the teacher, which decreased the time that children were able to devote to their work. In this environment teachers found it difficult to engage in extended challenging conversations of the kind likely to stimulate new ideas among their pupils. Studies of teachers in small primary schools (Galton and Patrick, 1990) found that nearly 40 per cent of exchanges between teachers and pupils during individualized instruction did not last longer than five seconds. As a consequence, smaller portions of time were available for providing feedback in the presence of the pupil. Indeed, such teachers were often forced to mark the books without the pupil being present and to hand them back without an extended oral comment.

Thus what went on in the primary classroom was, in fact, a complete reversal of what critics believed to be happening. Whereas the public was being encouraged to believe that in the informal primary classroom (that is, classrooms where children sat in groups and were given individual assignments rather than taught as a whole class) pupils were never told anything but left to find things out for themselves, the opposite was taking place and for the most part children were being told what to do more frequently than under any other form of organization.

It is important to grasp this point at the outset of the book. The weakness of individualized approaches to teaching and learning in the primary classroom appears not to lay in the method itself. Properly applied, teachers using such approaches can achieve comparable results to those preferring to teach children in larger groups. What prevents the method from being effective, under typical classroom conditions, is the dependency on the teacher that many children exhibit. As a result, the time available for teaching is often used inappropriately. To use individualized approaches successfully, teachers, therefore, have to overcome what, in its extreme form, has been called 'learned helplessness' by psychologists. Whole-class teaching appears to work, in part, because it allows these dependent pupils to exercise this dependency undetected by the teacher. When, for example, questions are being asked, they can keep their hand down and try to avoid the teacher's eye.

Common sense would suggest that a balance needs to be struck between the different kinds of organizational strategies which teachers deploy in the classroom. The issue of the over-dependency of some children on the teacher in many primary classrooms does not, therefore, become irrelevant even if the majority of teachers shift their current practice in ways which match the recommendations emerging from recent reports in favour of more whole-class teaching. Indeed, the issue of pupil independence and how to foster it assumes increasing importance once the third possibility for organizing pupils in the classroom, namely the use of grouping, is considered. Here the results of the ORACLE studies and other similar work, particularly that of Mortimore et al. (1988) and Tizard et al. (1988) are particularly relevant. These latter two studies covered both junior and early years classes and found similar patterns of organization to that described in ORACLE. The most striking of all findings concerned what Galton et al. (1980) termed the 'asymmetry of classroom interaction'. Put simply, this asymmetry referred to the observation that children sat in groups, usually consisting of four or five pupils of mixed sex, but worked at individual assignments. Consequently, while teachers engaged in one-to-one interactions with particular pupils in turn, for the majority of the school day, the remainder generally worked on their own without any contact with the teacher. This pattern was a consequence of the fact that there were on average 30 pupils but one teacher for each class.

One obvious way of compensating for this isolation would be for the pupils, when the teacher was elsewhere, to support each other in their work, either in pairs through peer tutoring (Goodlad and Hurst, 1989) or by working together in a collaborative group. Such activities, at least in theory, allow pupils to develop skills of oracy and debate as well as social skills of tolerance and courtesy when listening to another person's point of view without interruption. Conversations of this kind take on a greater importance when set against the fact that during whole-class teaching the majority of pupils do not participate in the exchanges but listen to the teacher talking for nearly 75 per cent of the time. It is precisely because most teachers recognize the advantages and disadvantages of whole-class teaching and the need to provide opportunities for pupils to engage in extended conversation, that they usually reply, when asked about their preferred teaching strategies, 'I use mixed methods'.

Matching Tasks to Teaching

This response, however, begs two important questions. The first concerns the curriculum activities for which each method is used. Both the ORACLE research and that of Mortimore and more recent work by Galton and Patrick (1990) in small schools, has shown for example that whole-class teaching is largely used for humanities or, within the present National Curriculum structure, for history and geography. Individual assignments are largely allocated when the topics involve English grammar or mathematical computation. Group work is more often used with science or art. The important question is, therefore, whether the curriculum task is appropriately matched to the chosen teaching strategy. In Chapter 5 this question will be examined in some detail.

A second issue concerns the proportion of time during which the different strategies are used. Logically, this should be partly related to the curriculum task. For example, in primary schools the greatest amount of curriculum time is given to English and mathematics. Since English and mathematics tend mainly to be taught through the use of individual instruction, it follows that the proportion of time devoted to individual instruction should be high relative to the use of other teaching strategies. However, matters are not quite so straightforward, since in many classrooms the time devoted to the use of different instructional strategies does not closely correspond to the curriculum coverage. Group work provides a particular example of this phenomena. In the typical primary classroom the smallest proportion of time (around

8 per cent) is devoted to cooperative group activity, compared to 15 per cent of time to whole-class teaching and 77 per cent of time to individual instructions marking and monitoring. Yet next to whole-class teaching, where children spend 90 per cent of the time listening to the teacher, the highest levels of on-task behaviour occur among collaborative groups. Since teachers would rate as their highest priority a classroom where most of the children are engaged for most of the time in purposeful activity – group work meets this need – it might be assumed that it would be a popular teaching strategy. The fact that children spend most of their time being taught in ways which mitigate against this goal of purposeful activity suggests there may be quite complex factors at work which cause a teacher to favour one kind of teaching strategy over another.

Alexander *et al.* (1989) and Alexander (1991) have found similar patterns of classroom organization in inner-city schools compared to rural primary schools (Galton and Patrick, 1990). Alexander's research will be the subject of detailed scrutiny in Chapter 4. But what can be said at the conclusion of this brief review is that all the research of the past two decades shows the patterns of organization and teaching developed in the late 1960s and early 1970s, to cope with the change from streamed to mixed ability classes, exhibit remarkable stability and strong resistance to attempts at modification. These facts were well documented by the early 1980s, yet outside the research community there was little public debate on the implications of these findings. The then Schools Council, for example, specifically advised teachers to treat this research with caution (Schools Council, 1983, p.116) on the grounds that the individual studies were based upon small samples. In so doing they chose to ignore the fact that these various studies, nevertheless, replicated each other, thus considerably increasing the likelihood that results could safely be generalized to the whole population of primary schools. Neither had Her Majesty's Inspectors, although conducting surveys of both primary schools (HMI, 1978) and middle schools (HMI, 1983), much to say in later publications about ways of improving the effectiveness of teaching. By and large the attention of the Inspectorate during the early 1980s was directed to issues of curriculum balance and continuity.

While it may be true that some LEAs attempted to use the findings from this body of research to improve the quality of teaching and learning in their schools, such programmes were, for the most part, opportunistic and lacked the coherence which might have been provided through a national initiative. Throughout this time the same national Inspectorate continually visited primary schools and issued reports.

They also visited schools and colleges of education and reported, for the most part favourably, on the training of new teachers as part of the accreditation procedures set up by the Council for Accreditation for Teacher Education (CATE) (HMI, 1982, 1987). Until fairly recently, therefore, this lack of any serious interest in pedagogy seems to have received the seal of official approval. Given this indifference, it may seem, to the disinterested observer, somewhat unfair to find that local authorities and training institutions are now being told that they must accept major responsibility for failing to improve the effectiveness of teaching and learning in our primary schools.

Making a Curriculum

Twenty years or so ago, mention of the school curriculum in the British context generated discussions about problems in organizing the school timetable or the construction of a syllabus. At the time, little attention was given to either the educational aims which determined why this topic rather than another should be taught, or to the intended outcomes of this teaching. More relevant to the theme of this book, there was no serious debate about the most effective way of achieving these outcomes.

In the period immediately following the second world war there still existed a consensus among both political parties, supported by informed public opinion, that the purpose of the secondary school curriculum was to bring pupils with sufficient ability to a point where they could either study a specific subject in depth at a university or enter directly into a recognized profession. Those pupils with less academic potential were equipped with the necessary practical skills to enter the job market at age 14. It was felt that these different functions, the one academic the other utilitarian, were better carried out in separate schools. The task of the primary school was to prepare pupils for these different forms of secondary provision by giving each child a sound education in basic skills, coupled with a smattering of general knowledge, including an appreciation of the wonders of nature. At the end of this primary phase it was then thought feasible to determine, by means of testing, broad differences in pupils' academic potential. These differences were then used to inform decisions about each pupil's future secondary school career.

This consensus began to break down in the early 1960s with the collation of evidence from difference sources showing that the system of selection was itself inefficient, particularly the use of an examination at age 11 as a predictor of a pupil's future achievement. At the same time, the rigid divisions between practical and academic education were increasingly seen to be a major handicap in the nation's attempt to expand the number of pupils with scientific and technological expertise. C. P. Snow's famous 'Two Cultures' Rede Lecture and the Dainton's Committee's (1968) investigation of the swing away from science subjects among grammar school pupils helped speed reform, not only of the science curriculum itself but also of the ways in which school science was taught. This reform movement, sponsored by both the Nuffield Foundation and the Schools Council, was gradually extended into the primary phase, one example being the Nuffield Junior Science Project.

This first wave of British curriculum reform followed on closely from similar developments in the United States; there, however, interest in the process of curriculum making as a serious component of educational enquiry was much further advanced. In the United Kingdom the first published book on the subject was D. K. Wheeler's (1967) *Curriculum Process* which relied heavily on the research carried out in the United States in the previous two decades. Wheeler's book was intended to illuminate such questions as, 'Why should we teach this topic rather than that?', 'Who should have access to this knowledge?' and, 'How should parts of this curriculum be interrelated in order to create a coherent whole?' Questions of this kind clearly relate to what are perceived at the time to be a society's needs, as well as those of individuals within that society. The more the needs of the society are held to be of greater importance the stronger will be the tendency to determine the curriculum centrally rather than leaving the choice of topics and methods to individual schools.

In the primary phase, over recent years, there exists a common trend, among all industrialized societies, to evolve a curriculum which promotes modern scientific and technological development while at the same time coping with greater cultural diversity because of increased migration across national borders. Other factors, for example the shift in population from rural areas and an increased understanding of the potential of handicapped pupils, have also given rise to a shared perspective which enabled European educators to agree on common aims when meeting under the auspices of the Council of Europe at Vaduz (CDCC, 1982). Questions of how such a curriculum should be constructed and presented are, however, much more difficult to answer because their resolution involves beliefs about the relative importance of different forms of knowledge as well as beliefs about the most effective way for children to acquire such knowledge. When Wheeler's book was published, curriculum building was chiefly concerned with the relative importance accorded to the different disciplines and the balance between a general and a specialized education. For the most part, a transmission model of knowledge was assumed whereby, through increased specialization, pupils came to know as much as their teachers. Those who showed the greatest ability were then encouraged to go on and extend the frontiers of knowledge in the particular discipline through further research.

Ideology and the Curriculum: 1970–80

By the early 1970s, however, this model of curriculum making was increasingly being challenged. First, sociologists began to question the view that some forms of knowledge were of more value than others. Young (1971) argued, for example, that knowledge was socially constructed. Certain activities were, therefore, deemed of more importance than others because they afforded a way of justifying the advancement of one group of members within society in comparison with another. For Young, the selection of certain kinds of examination question, for example, did not signify that the knowledge tested was of greater importance than that covered in topics which were excluded. The value of the chosen questions was that they discriminated efficiently between individuals who were to be offered advancement and those who were not. That was why examination results correlated highly with social class and why the most advantaged groups within society were able to reproduce the same advantages from one generation to the next.

Even more important than the debate about the social construction of knowledge has been the extension of the meaning associated with the word 'culture'. In the eighteenth and nineteenth centuries culture was equated with 'a general state or habit of the mind', having a close association with the idea of human perfection with an emphasis on the intellectual and the spiritual. Raymond Williams (1961) however, in his work *Culture and Society*, put forward the view that culture should be identified with *the whole way of life of a society* which in this century has become increasingly associated in western thought with ideas about the nature of social relationships. A key factor in this change has been the creation of the new political democratic movements which have arisen in response to industrialism.

Williams' ideas have been taken up in the work of Denis Lawton (1975) for whom curriculum content represents a selection of the culture defined as 'the fabric of ideals, beliefs, skills, tools, aesthetic objects, methods of thinking, customs and institutions into which each member of a society is born' (Reynolds and Skilbeck, 1976, p.5). Lawton takes issue with Young's (1971) view of the arbitrariness and artificiality of subject boundaries, arguing that there are other factors involved beside social ones and 'it is at least possible that some kinds of knowledge are superior in some meaningful way to other kinds of knowledge' (Lawton, 1975, p.62). For Lawton, the idea of a common culture leads naturally to the notion of a 'common curriculum'. He rejects the assumptions inherent in the construction of a curriculum based upon discrete disciplines with the choice of either academic or practical options dependent on a pupil's ability.

Throughout the late 1970s and early 1980s, Lawton's views became increasingly influential in the debate about curriculum entitlement, balance and continuity. Documents of the period, for example the reports of Her Majesty's Inspectors (DES, 1980, 1983, 1985a), increasingly promoted the idea of the pupil's entitlement to a broad and balanced common curriculum based upon Lawton's cultural framework.

This philosophical approach to curriculum making has been called 'reconstructionism' which Malcolm Skilbeck (1982, p.11) summarizes in the following manner. First, it assumes that education is one of the major forces for bringing about planned change within a society. Second, it states that educational processes must be distinguished from other social processes which are also intended to bring about change, such as party political activity, commercial advertising or mass entertainment. An important function of the educational process is therefore to help pupils cope with these other determinants of social change in ways that safeguard the community's interests. Third, it questions the idea of knowledge for its own sake and stresses the importance of treating information and evidence critically. There is an emphasis on learning through the use of problem-solving strategies. Finally, reconstructionism is based upon the assumption that an individual can best realize his or her full potential within the structure of a democratic society so that values of citizenship, social cooperation and community are continually stressed during teaching.

It is not difficult to see why a curriculum underpinned by the idea of a 'social democratic culture' should have received general approval at this time. Despite the rhetoric, the main differences between the two major political parties chiefly concerned means rather than ends. This consensus was particularly strong in respect of social policy issues such as education, health and support for the elderly and other low-income groups.

Ideology and the Curriculum: 1980–90

All this changed, however, with the election of Margaret Thatcher to the leadership of the Conservative Party followed by her victory in the 1979 general election. Prior to this change in leadership, a growing minority within the Conservative Party had begun to criticize many of the basic assumptions which lay behind the creation of the modern welfare state. The main source of these new ideas was the Centre for Policy Studies, set up by Sir Keith Joseph and Margaret Thatcher when in opposition. The centre published a series of papers which argued that the great public services should be subject to the same market forces as govern the operations of private industry. In the early years following 1979, the main targets were the nationalized industries but by the mid-1980s, increasing attention was being paid to education. As Tomlinson (1992, p.47) argues, 'it was the methods not the objectives that were new'. The traditional processes of consultation were abandoned or curtailed, one regular strategy being to issue documents over the summer holiday period. Members of consultative bodies were no longer appointed to represent a broad range of interests but were nominated by government to ensure that policy changes would be driven through regardless. Government grants to LEAs were earmarked and payment subject to the attainment of specific performance indicators, a device which according to Tomlinson (1992, p.47) 'simultaneously marginalised the LEAs and began the forging of the tools of direct central control of schools'. Gradually Lawton's idea of a 'common curriculum' became a vehicle for enhancing central control of the educational process rather than ensuring pupil entitlement. From this agenda emerged the 1988 Education Act and with it the creation of the National Curriculum.

Despite these changes, demands for further reform have emanated from lobbies such as the Centre for Policy Studies (Hillgate Group, 1989; Lawlor, 1988). Many of these writers continually direct their attack at the proposition that the faults within the educational system can largely be attributed to a strong markedly 'left of centre' viewpoint which has become entrenched within the educational establishment, both in the colleges of education and the local authority advisory service. While it could be argued that some of the most articulate writing on curriculum issues within the last decade has emerged from a 'left of centre' group who have been labelled 'reconceptualists' (Lawn and Barton, 1981), the extent of their influence, particularly in schools, is more debatable.

These reconceptualist writers have disagreed strongly with Lawton's ideas, particularly his notion of a common curriculum based upon a common culture. They argue, on the basis of empirical evidence about the practice of comprehensive schooling (Ball, 1981; Willis, 1977) and of primary schooling (Sharp and Green, 1975), that far from extending opportunities to working-class children, the common curriculum has been a device for maintaining the existing highly stratified class system. For example, developments supported by Lawton and Skilbeck, such as the replacement of conventional examinations by continuous assessment of topic work, have, it is claimed, increased the advantages of middle-class children who have available additional resources in the form of highly articulate parents with access to a greater range of sources of information. What, therefore, were heralded at the time as important reforms such as the use of Mode 3 Assessment in the CSE were, according to these critics, just another means of ensuring that working-class children were prevented from demonstrating their full potential.

These reconceptualist writers also rejected Lawton's key principle that it is possible to change society through education. They argued that one needed to change society first in order to bring about change in schools and for this reason teachers must take a political stance against intended government reforms (Clark and Davies, 1981). Similar arguments had been developed in the United States in the writings of Bowles and Gintis (1976) and Michael Apple (1982). However, it must be doubted whether the ideas of these curriculum theorists have exerted any major practical influence since their arguments would suggest that, in the absence of strong revolutionary forces within society, there is little that teachers can do except to raise the awareness of their pupils about the class structures in society and the distribution of political power.

There is therefore likely to be very little difference in the academic content of the curriculum whatever the ideological stance taken by curriculum developers. This may be illustrated by reference to a frequently used activity at the top end of the middle school where children are asked to investigate the best buy amongst a range of domestic bleaches, including the one regularly advertised on television with the claim that 'it kills all known germs'. The exercise relies on the chemical properties of a purple-coloured acidified solution of a substance called potassium permanganate. A solution of this substance becomes colourless in the presence of a bleaching agent. A fair test can be carried out if permanganate solution, of a known strength, is carefully added to fixed volumes of appropriately diluted samples of various bleach solutions until it is in excess. Clearly the more permanganate solution required to re-establish a permanent purple colour, the stronger and the more effective will be the bleach. Given the price of each container of bleach and its volume, it is now possible to work out the effectiveness of each product in terms of its cost per unit of volume.

Now both reconstructionist and reconceptualist teachers might wish to link this knowledge about a particular chemical reaction to wider issues connected to the marketing of these products. For Lawton, since advertising is 'part of our way of life', it would be important to link the chemical knowledge to the wider issue of how advertising influences public opinion, given that the market share of a particular bleaching product would probably be more highly correlated with the advertising costs than its effectiveness. A reconceptualist teacher, however, might wish to take the debate further and ask why the public was not protected from such advertising. They might point to the fact that the body set up to safeguard the public from inaccurate advertising was a self-regulating one, leading directly into a further discussion about the exercise of power within society. The aim of such a lesson would be to demonstrate how processes which, on the surface appear democratic, are subject, in subtle ways, to a high degree of control and manipulation.

The net effect of both lessons based on these approaches, however, would hardly be likely to bring pupils out onto the streets to man the barricades! More importantly, in each lesson the teacher could only achieve the aims by maintaining the highest academic standards. However, in the case of someone concerned only with imparting subject knowledge it would be possible to conclude the lesson even if the experiment failed. In such cases, many teachers have been known to substitute a set of parallel results from an example in the textbook! Pupils could still work on this substituted data in mastering the principles of the chemical process. But the teacher, hoping to influence the attitudes and beliefs of the pupils, could only hope to convince them if the data obtained were regarded as 'real' and genuine. For this to happen the experiment must work well and hence much greater care needs to be taken both in its preparation and execution. Only if the pupils discover for themselves that the public buys less effective bleach products would they be likely to become interested in the wider issue of advertising standards and their control.

Curriculum Hybridization: A Limiting Factor

There is another important factor which reduces the influence of ideology on what is taught and how it is taught. The work of Kliebard (1986) has convincingly demonstrated that, in nearly a century of American education, no ideological group ever succeeded in imposing a curriculum on schools based upon their particular principles. This is because within teaching there is a tendency to resist making changes to existing classroom practice when it appears to be working moderately well. As a result, rather than replace one curriculum by another, schools tend to adapt the most recent innovation to fit in with the previous initiatives whenever possible. The resulting product is thus a mixture of the old and the new. This process of blending different reforms, which Kliebard terms 'hybridization', is a recurring feature of all curriculum innovation, particularly the 'top-down' kind developed by experts and then offered to schools after a period of consultation and possibly trial. However, Fullan and Hargreaves (1992) are particularly critical of such approaches, arguing that such reforms,

> However noble, sophisticated or enlightened ... come to nothing if teachers don't adopt them in their own classroom and if they don't translate them into effective practice. (p.21)

Failure to take the full implications of this statement into account has meant that most previous attempts at 'top-down' educational reforms, similar to those of the National Curriculum, have not been implemented in schools in the manner hoped for by the curriculum developers. Fullan and Hargreaves note that there are many reasons for this lack of success. The complexity of the problems that the reform is intended to solve is often ignored and, consequently, the time-lines set are often unrealistic. Because policy makers generally require quick results, there is a tendency towards what Fullan and Hargreaves (1992, p.22) call 'fadism' and 'quick fix' solutions. Structural changes, such as redefining the curriculum or increasing the amounts of assessment and testing are often preferred, although such strategies 'not only fail to motivate teachers to implement fully these (hybridization) improvements but also alienate them from participating in further reform'.

Fullan (1992) extends these arguments when discussing the role of the headteacher in promoting innovation. He notes that externally generated top-down procedures, which it is assumed provide a framework for the head in the role of curriculum manager, often 'backfire' because they induce feelings of dependency. Believing that 'somebody out there' is in control and therefore must have anticipated their problems, the headteacher tends to look outside his/her personal resources for solutions to the difficulties experienced when attempting to make the reforms work in a particular context. But as Patterson et al. (1986) have argued, the planner's ability to anticipate problems is limited because 'out there' 'is not too rational'. Most social systems do not operate in rational ways, which curriculum planners appear to think they do. Nevertheless, although society does not follow an orderly logic but a complex one, this is 'understandable and amenable to influence' (Fullan, 1992, p.16). Thus the non-rational world is not necessarily a non-sensical one. Fullan notes that those who think otherwise and hold to a rational approach usually begin by believing that changes in the procedures, particularly in the curriculum content and its assessment, will lead to improvements in practice. According to Fullan, when this 'if-then' philosophy fails, the only recourse left is to shift to an 'if-only' position and to argue that,

> If only schools would tighten up rules and regulations improved discipline will follow. If only teachers were given clear directives, then improved teaching will follow. (Fullan, 1992, p.17)

In contrast, advocates for the non-rational model claim that this

> 'if-then' and 'if-only' model is wishful thinking. Organisations do not always behave in a logical, predictable manner. Rather than spending organisational energy trying to conform to wishful thinking, the non-rational model allows us to invest our energy into devising solutions that will work, given reality. (Fullan, 1992, p.17, quoting Patterson et al., 1986)

Fullan's analysis is particularly relevant to the National Curriculum since in its design it bears all the hallmarks of a 'failed innovation', as predicted by Fullan and Hargreaves (1992). It is the non-rational nature of curriculum innovation, increasingly evident as social systems become more complex, that gives rise to hybridization. Because these irrational tendencies are not well understood by schools, and therefore not well managed, the mixture of the old and the new is often unsatisfactory. This is particularly true of the classroom where the greatest resistance to change is often to be found. Teachers are naturally reluctant to give up existing practices for innovations that they neither understand nor feel part of. The effects of this hybridization on primary practice in the aftermath of the National Curriculum will, therefore, be an important theme in this book.

This present chapter has, however, now brought us to the point where we can begin to consider some of the curriculum issues which have taken on a greater urgency as a result of the National Curriculum and the associated government reforms. These changes in the primary curriculum appear to have arisen partly as a reaction to the perceived threat from the views of a minority of teachers and educationalists. Since these views have generally been expressed in the more radical educational publications, it is doubtful whether their influence went far beyond the minority of teacher readers who suscribe to these few journals. That there were problems within the primary curriculum as it existed before the 1988 Education Act must be admitted. That these problems arose because of the ideological commitment of educationalists and teachers will be disputed. This caveat is an important one, since the preferred solution for bringing about improvements differs according to one's judgements about the causes of the problem. This should become clearer as the argument develops in the following chapters.

Chapter 2
Do we Need a National Curriculum

Since the introduction of the first orders in the core subjects at Key Stage 1 during 1989, the answer from teachers to the question posed in the title of the chapter would seem increasingly to be, 'Yes, but not the one we've got'. At the same time there are mixed feelings at the prospect of further proposed changes. There are worries that, although the demands have been reduced, 'the content's still the same', so it's going to be, 'just more difficult to decide whether you've done something or not because there are so many bits' (Webb, 1993, p.53), while others, while accepting that the curriculum is overloaded, are, 'fed up with changes. Really, I'm fed up of doing all this work and then somebody else saying, "Oh. No"' (ibid.).

Looking back, there is now a tendency to attribute these problems of curriculum overload, and all the other difficulties experienced during the implementation phase, not only to the rapid introduction of the 1988 Education Reform Act but also to the lack of any consensus about the need for curriculum reform. Yet the idea of a National Curriculum was clearly foreshadowed in a series of government papers throughout the 1980s. Beginning with *A Framework for the School Curriculum* (DES, 1980) which contained recommended percentages of time to be devoted to particular subjects, and continuing throughout the mid-1980s with Her Majesty's Inspectors' *Curriculum Matters* series together with the White Paper, *Better Schools* (DES, 1985b), there emerged an increasing emphasis on the notion of an 'entitlement' for all pupils. This required schools to provide a *broad* introduction to a wide range of areas of experience, knowledge and skills; to ensure a carefully *balanced* allocation of time between different curriculum areas; and to teach a range of topics in ways which were *relevant* to the pupil's own experience and to the young person's future adult life and the world of employment. A fourth requirement that the curriculum should be *differentiated* required that the teaching should match the needs and abilities of different children.

What was also of crucial importance, as Pring (1989) argues, was that in all the reports there was an assumption that these entitlements could only be achieved through the exercise of a greater degree of control by central government of what was taught in schools. This was in sharp contrast to the position in the 1960s and 70s where central government, while issuing broad guidelines, relied on the LEAs and schools to interpret these recommendations in ways which suited local conditions. However, surveys carried out during this period, mainly by HMI and by researchers, clearly showed the unevenness of provision, not only across local authorities but between and within schools within each local authority. Such differences chiefly concerned the amount of time spent in school, the proportions of this time devoted to different subjects and the provision of resources used to support this teaching and learning. By 1988, therefore, the idea of a National Curriculum which would reduce the disparity in the various learning experiences which children encountered from different teachers in different schools was generally accepted. Already, during the early 1980s, many local authorities were encouraging schools to undertake full-scale curriculum reviews (Willcocks and Eustace, 1980) in pursuit of this objective.

Yet by 1990, when the first evidence began to emerge concerning the implementation of the National Curriculum in the core subjects, it would seem, according to one review, that

> For class teachers, delivering the broad and balanced curriculum had become, or would become, not a dream but a nightmare. It was simply not manageable even for experienced and able teachers. (Campbell, 1993, p.23)

Now, with the evidence from Key Stage 1, on which Campbell's judgement was made, supported by studies of implementation at Key Stages 1 and 2 (NCC, 1993; OFSTED, 1993a, 1993b; Webb, 1993), it has been necessary to call for a full and radical revision of the whole enterprise, culminating in the publication of the Dearing Reports (1993a, 1993b) and the setting up once more of various subject committees to review the whole curriculum. The National Curriculum Council has retreated from its base in York and has once again merged with SEAC to become the Schools Curriculum and Assessment Authority (SCAA). The full cost of the experimentation during the past six years has yet to be assessed. Not only were the financial costs considerable (the National Curriculum Council's budget alone ran to several million pounds a year with an estimated total bill of £45 million) but there have also been the costs associated with the stress, frustration and disillusion induced among practising teachers.

It is said that at an early stage, a certain government minister, when speaking to one of the NCC subject committees, likened the implementation process to the Falklands campaign, where one had to push forward as fast as possible in the confident knowledge that, while there would be some local difficulties, everyone would eventually reach the desired goal. On the National Curriculum journey, however, there seems to have been a number of 'Bluff Cove' disasters before schools have sighted Port Stanley. Time will reveal whether, apart from the teachers, the ultimate sufferers have been the generation of children on whom the initial experiments were conducted.

In looking back over this period, this chapter will examine how, despite the initial enthusiasm and general agreement that a National Curriculum was required, the final outcome for primary education, in particular, appears to have been so unsatisfactory. Having conducted this analysis, it will then go on to see whether the solutions proposed by Dearing (1993b) are likely to improve the situation, or whether the fundamental flaws in the way the National Curriculum was originally designed and implemented will prevent the development of an 'entitlement curriculum' which was the initial objective of the reform.

1988: The Interim Primary Committee

Shortly after the passing of the 1988 Education Reform Act and the appointment of Duncan Graham, the former Chief Education Officer for Suffolk, as the first chief executive to the National Curriculum Council, a working party with the title, 'Interim Primary Committee', was set up. The Committee, which was chaired by the then Chief Education Officer of Cumbria, was responsible directly to the National Curriculum Council. Its remit was to suggest strategies by which primary schools might implement the demands of the National Curriculum as determined by the recently constituted subject committees.

The Interim Primary Committee was dominated by local authority representatives, senior advisers and teachers, with two academics (one a token black). From the government's side there was one representative from the then Department of Education and Science and two HMI members. The teachers chosen appeared to be either those whose work was previously known to members of the National Curriculum Council or who had attracted the attention of government ministers during recent visits to primary schools. Similarly, the appointment of the one white academic arose because he had conducted part of a recent curriculum project on small schools within the chairman's county and had met with him on a number of occasions. These National Curriculum Council committees were, therefore, very unlike the earlier bodies which were formed by the Schools Council, where the majority of places were taken up by nominations. Although there still was an attempt to balance different representative groups when forming these committees, membership was largely through patronage. Subsequently, some members of this Interim Primary Committee were given additional responsibilities within the remaining committee structure of the National Curriculum Council, including membership of the Council itself. This additional involvement appeared to arise mainly as a result of two factors: first, an ability to produce written materials under great time pressure and second, the willingness only to prosecute a line of argument within the Committee that did not conflict too strongly with the guidelines being developed by government ministers and the chief executive. Reports of the development of these guidelines can be found in Duncan Graham's own account of the creation of the National Curriculum, following his resignation (some would describe it as dismissal) as chief executive (Graham, 1993).

Initially the Committee had very clear ideas about the areas where it wished to offer advice to the Secretary of State about needed developments in primary practice. First, it was recognized that schools had to look closely at their organization in order to maximize the time available for learning. To achieve this goal, schools would be required to carry out a 'time audit' similar to that recommended by the Inner London Education Authority (ILEA) to its schools by the then Senior Primary Adviser, Barbara MacGilchrist, herself a member of the Interim Primary Committee. Second, there was a clear recognition that without the development of a thematic approach it would be impossible to cope with the demands being made of primary teachers across the various curriculum subjects. Initially, a considerable amount of time was spent on this matter, looking at ways at which the traditional 'topic web', based on lesson topics, could be replaced with schemes which mapped out tasks in terms of achievable attainment targets from different subject elements. These deliberations aimed to change the current practice where, generally, mathematics and English were taught as single subjects and topic work was confined to the humanities. The new approach sought to link practical work in subjects like geography and science with mathematics, thus reversing the findings of various research studies (for example, Galton and Patrick, 1990) which showed that science tasks rarely involved any measurement of length or time. There was also recognition that, in the past, guidance on appropriate teaching strategies had been so general as to be of little use to the practitioner in the classroom. What was now required was a series of clear statements which linked appropriate teaching strategies to the intellectual demands of any set task. Such an analysis might properly address such questions as when direct instruction was best used or when collaborative group work was to be preferred.

After almost a year of these discussions, some progress had been made, particularly with respect to time audits and on the question of dealing with the development of topic work, including aspects of mathematics and language. Indeed, parts of the draft report were felt to require only minor changes. This work came to an abrupt halt, however, in mid-June when Duncan Graham joined the meeting and informed members of the Interim Primary Committee that the report was urgently required by then Secretary of State for Education, Kenneth Baker. The rest of the drafting would therefore be taken over by one of Council's staff. When some members protested at this procedure, and asked whether they would have an opportunity to see the final draft, they were informed that within the given time-scale there was no possibility of bringing the report back to the Committee before submitting it to the Council. Under pressure, however, Duncan Graham finally agreed that three members of the Interim Primary Committee could have an opportunity to study the report over the weekend and to fax their comments back to the National Curriculum Council offices by lunch-time on Monday. In the event, one of these three scrutineers, a local authority adviser (the two others were an HMI and a teacher), read extracts of the report to others members of the Committee over the telephone so that they could add their comments. However, in the nature of things, it was always likely that the person responsible for the final draft should adopt the expedient of dealing with different suggestions of the three scrutineers by either omitting all reference to the matter or redrafting in a form of words which was capable of the widest possible interpretation. Inevitably, therefore, what emerged, particularly in the discussion of pedagogic issues, appeared bland, with exhortations to teachers to note that 'the proposals had implications for forming groups' or that 'teachers would need to look again at the forms of record keeping employed'. The report was now concerned to *advise* on what should be done. Little guidance was given on possible strategies for implementing this *advice*.

By the time the Interim Primary Committee assembled for their final meeting, the report had already gone from the Curriculum Council to the then Department of Education and Science. There was some discussion of how best use could be made of the document by LEAs and schools, but the general feeling was one of disappointment and a sense of an opportunity wasted. The chief executive again attended in order to thank the Committee members for their work. Some members expressed concern about the report and the way Committee members had been treated. When one of those present said that he was embarrassed to be associated with a document that had such little intellectual rigour, he was informed that the report was the property and the responsibility of the National Curriculum Council and not this Committee. The Interim Committee was merely advisory and the National Curriculum Council was at liberty either to accept or reject its advice. When the Committee moved on from the actual report to suggest that within the new structures now being considered a Primary Committee ought to be maintained, this advice was also politely but firmly rejected. Members were told that it would be sufficient to have primary representatives on the subject panels.

While there were problems with the timetables of other Committees, also forcing them to produce reports under severe time pressure, none was quite so dramatic as that recounted above. The more crucial decision, however, was not to maintain a specific primary group to oversee developments at Key Stages 1 and 2. There was now no group within the Council capable of controlling the emphasis on subject content which would inevitably develop out of the concerns of the majority of members with secondary school backgrounds who formed the various subject panels.

It is not difficult to see why these secondary-dominated panels were concerned to be highly prescriptive on matters of content. During the previous decade, studies of the transfer process between primary and secondary schools (Gorwood, 1994) had attempted to improve curriculum continuity, and thereby reduce the levels of frustration experienced by secondary teachers when coping with the diversity of practice emanating from their primary feeder schools. The structure and composition of the National Curriculum subject panels now allowed secondary representatives to address this problem to their own advantage. By defining the curriculum content through the detailed *programmes of study*, and the expected curriculum outcomes by numerous *statements of attainment* within each programme of study, it became possible, for the first time since the 11-plus examination, to visualize a system where children coming into the secondary school would, in theory, have covered exactly the same topics in similar ways. This assumption was based on the belief that when these statements of attainment were translated into assessment tasks, primary teachers would 'teach to the tests'. As a consequence, planning a curriculum around the needs of particular children or taking into account local influences as a way of stimulating the pupils' interest and motivation – perceived characteristics of existing primary practice – would become more difficult. Thus the emerging view within the National Curriculum Council's subject committees, that one of the main benefits of the reformed primary curriculum should be to ensure continuity and progression into the secondary stage, not only satisfied representatives of the secondary schools but also those members of the National Curriculum Council who had been nominated by the government. In particular, those from the 'New Right', whom Ball (1990, p.6) describes as 'hardline old humanists' and 'cultural restorationists', regarded the overwhelming emphasis on subject content, backed up by regular testing, as heralding the long awaited victory over 'Plowdenism'.

1989: A Framework for the Primary Curriculum

One further consequence of the decision not to continue with a more permanent form of the Interim Primary Committee was that when its report was finally published, under the title, *A Framework for the Primary Curriculum* (NCC, 1989), there was no group within the body of the National Curriculum Council with an interest in promoting its dissemination. Given its overall blandness it was not therefore surprising that the report made little impact either in the press or in the schools. Only the issue of time audits, among those originally identified, was addressed in any great detail. There was no mention of pedagogy. The body of the text was divided into four main sections: planning the curriculum; continuity within the curriculum; implementing the curriculum; and the education of children under 5. This latter section was introduced because of concern among HMI committee members that with the introduction of Key Stage 1, there would be an attempt in some schools to teach versions of this programme within the nursery classes in order to give pupils additional advantages when it came to taking the SATs at age 7.

On planning, schools were recommended to carry out a curriculum audit in each of the core and foundation subjects, to analyse the use of time and to decide on the acquisition and deployment of resources. This would then lead to the establishment of a National Curriculum Development Plan. The *Framework* recognized that it would 'be impossible to deliver all subjects in simple strands in a twenty-five or twenty-seven hour week. The issue for schools will be how to combine subject stands in coherent ways' (para 2.12, p.8). However, apart from referring to examples found in other consultative reports such as *English (5–11)*, no precise advice on how this could be done was offered. Curriculum continuity, it was claimed, would now be more readily achievable because,

the National Curriculum enables curriculum continuity to be established by providing a clear framework, requiring class teachers to build on the previous year's work, offers a common language for all schools and requires assessment both within and at the end of each Key Stage which informs decisions about work at the next stage. (para 2.16, p.8)

This statement was not in the early versions but was added at the final drafting stage when 'ownership' of the document had been taken away from the Interim Primary Committee members.

The *Framework* reaffirmed that school management was fundamentally about managing the curriculum, but remained ambivalent on how this planning exercise should be carried out. Within the *Framework* there was no mention of any recognized procedure for curriculum planning nor reference to any principles which might guide the process. Instead, the authors of the final draft resorted to cliché and generality, advising headteachers when engaged in planning for the National Curriculum that it would be 'counter productive to lose existing good practice' (nowhere defined in the report) but 'unhelpful for the learner to devise an unnecessary fragmented curriculum' (para 2.10, p.7). This latter assertion stems from HMI's repeatedly expressed view, reinforced in the Chief HMI's 1987/88 Report, that topic work more often than not lacked continuity and progression.

On implementing the curriculum within the classroom, the *Framework* offered little specific advice. Although identifying as key issues the grouping of pupils, the deployment of staff, management of resources, assessment, record keeping and monitoring the curriculum, there were few recommendations on what changes should be implemented. The officials of the National Curriculum Council seemed to share, along with their political masters, the optimistic belief that:

The clarity of the National Curriculum subject requirements and detailed information about pupils' achievements will allow teachers to make sure grouping arrangements are made appropriately. At all times the needs of the individual pupil should be given the highest priority. (para 3.3, p.11)

Here, in perhaps its clearest form, do we find stated the conviction that teachers would be forced to change their practice as the result of the increasing assessment demands within the core subjects. Yet it is typical of the report's drafting that it should attempt to soften the impact of the sentence by juxtaposing it with another about pupils' individual needs which nods in the direction of one of 'shibboleths' of progressive primary ideology! In another similar instance, the report states that there is a case for 'some increased subject specialist teaching', but almost immediately counters the implications of this statement by saying that schools should be concerned to avoid disruption and the consequent *fragmentation* of learning (para 3.3, p.13).

In treating the matter of assessment (pp. 14–15) the authors of the *Framework* document followed the TGAT report's reasoning in stressing the distinction between formative and summative assessment. The importance of record keeping was emphasized, but no guidance was given about how this should be done, apart from the comment that, 'the records which teachers keep at present will need to be restructured to show the attainment targets and the parts of the programmes of study taught to each pupil' (para 3.3, p.15).

In summary, on almost every issue the *Framework* identified the problem, set out the minimum demands of the National Curriculum which should be met, but left it to schools and to the teachers to work towards their own personal solutions. The model presented for promoting curriculum change appears to be, 'You, the teachers, are the experts and therefore we leave to you the task of developing the appropriate implementation strategies within the framework of the National Curriculum'.

It will become clear in Chapter 4, however, that some NCC members and the government believed that the *framework* was in effect a *straitjacket*. It was therefore unnecessary to enter into a meaningful dialogue with teachers concerning pedagogy, since the National Curriculum programmes of study, when allied to the attainment targets, would eventually force teachers into adopting more traditional approaches. For example, once pupils in any class had been identified as at level 1, 2, or possibly 3, the logic of grouping children by sets for specialist subject teaching appeared obvious. Hence, for some NCC members, the need for only a passing reference for teachers 'to make sure that grouping arrangements are made appropriately', and hence the growing anger and frustration expressed in private by some NCC officials when the attempts by SEAC to develop the required testing procedures began to alienate primary teachers from the entire reform programme.

The view that the NCC's strategy for implementing change was essentially correct, but that it was undermined by the difficulties within SEAC and by political subversion of government ministers (Graham, 1993), totally ignores the lessons to be learnt from previous experiments in curriculum innovation and reform, particularly the problem of 'hybridization' referred to at the end of the previous chapter. Like its chief executive, most of those appointed to key positions within the NCC came from local authority backgrounds, either from the advisory or administrative service. This itself was somewhat ironic, given that the need for a National Curriculum arose partly out of the failures of these same local authority representatives to innovate and implement previous curriculum developments successfully. Few, if any, of these NCC staff probably had any understanding of the principles of effective curriculum reform, such as those outlined in the previous chapter.

The evidence seems to point, therefore, to a mix of reasons for the decisions to proceed in the manner described. A naive view prevailed that if the aims of assessment were laudable, then building such appropriate attainment targets into the curriculum would ensure that teachers would change their practice in accordance with the requirements specified. In accounting for what followed during the next five years, this over-optimism, coupled with seeming neglect about the lessons to be learned from previous attempts to implement such major changes successfully, can also be placed alongside the desire of various Secretaries of State for Education to use their time at the Department of Education as a stepping stone to higher office (Simon, 1993). The net result, culminating in the need for a major overhaul of the programmes only four years after their initial introduction into schools, is unprecedented within the annals of curriculum reform.

1989: Introducing the National Curriculum

Once schools had started to cope with the various orders and statutory guidance, a number of research studies were commissioned by the various teacher organizations. Their purpose was to identify if any constraints existed to prevent the satisfactory implementation of the proposed curriculum changes. The first of these studies, funded by the Assistant Masters and Mistresses Association (AMMA) was carried out at the University of Warwick and concentrated on Key Stage 1 (Campbell and Neill, 1992).

This third report followed on from two other earlier surveys (Campbell and Neill, 1990, 1991). The data, mainly collected by questionnaire, dealt with the teachers' working conditions and their perceptions of the adequacy of time available for the various subjects in the National Curriculum. However, the timing of the third survey differed slightly from the previous two and allowed for information about the use of time for administering the standard assessment tasks.

In all three surveys, the teachers perceived the lack of time and large classes as the main obstacles to the implementation of the National Curriculum. Nearly three-quarters of the sample had less than ten hours per week support in the classroom from either a colleague or a non-teaching assistant, but rated such support as their main priority. This help was required most particularly for assessment and recording and for teaching smaller groups. Over the three years surveyed, teachers' workloads, during a typical working week in term, averaged 49.6, 54.6 and 52.4 hours (i.e., around ten hours per day). A breakdown of the 1992 figures showed that 18 hours per week were devoted to teaching, 14.5 to preparation, 13.6 to administration, 7.2 to professional development and 3.8 hours to other activities such as dealing with governors and running sport clubs and the orchestra. Administration included dealing with parents, setting up displays and liaison with outside agencies. Nearly half the time allowed for breaks during the working day was spent on such activity.

Furthermore, the proportion of time required for preparation and administration increased significantly with class size. Not unnaturally, the time devoted to teacher assessment and the SATs (39 hours over the ten weeks) was considerable and was greater than the time spent on geography, history, music and RE teaching combined. The greatest amount of teaching time was given to the core areas, English and mathematics. English received 29 per cent of the teaching time, mathematics 18 per cent and science and art 9 per cent each. Although these figures show about 6 per cent less time being devoted to mathematics than in the Curriculum Provision in Small Primary School (PRISMS) infants sample (Galton and Patrick, 1990), they are comparable with those of Tizard *et al.* (1988) in top infant London classes. However, the time devoted to English is about 8 per cent less than the PRISMS study found and much lower than the figures given by Tizard (although in the latter case the classes contained a sizeable proportion of children with second language problems). Using the criteria that at least half the teachers thought a subject had adequate time, only in English, mathematics, science, PE and art did teachers perceive there to be adequate provision.

The most significant finding to emerge from these three surveys was that teachers' workloads showed very little sign of diminishing over the three years in which they were monitored. This result directly contradicted the view expressed by NCC officials at the time of Campbell and Neill's first survey. NCC spokespersons had argued that it was only to be expected that teachers' workloads would increase during the initial period as they familiarized themselves with the procedures necessary to deliver the National Curriculum at Key Stage 1. Once this familiarization stage was complete, the effort and time involved should decrease significantly. However, not only did the teachers' workloads continue at an unacceptable level but they were also substantially higher than those recorded in the 1970s in a survey carried out by the National Foundation for Educational Research (Hilsum and Cane, 1971). The average workload in this 1970 study was 44.5 hours, compared to an average of around 54 hours across the three years spanning Campbell's and Neill's surveys. At the time, Hilsum and Cane's figures were thought to be inflated because their survey took place during a period when the teacher unions were pressing for dramatic increases in pay on the basis of increased productivity. Campbell and Neill (1992, p.57) concluded that the willingness of teachers to work long hours was the main reason for what success there was in delivering the National Curriculum at Key Stage 1. They attributed this 'conscientiousness' on the part of early years teachers to the fact that they are socialized by training and by their staffroom culture into vocational attitudes to their work. Campbell's and Neill's conclusion was that,

> Teachers cannot deliver all that they are legally required to do. The dilemma is intensified by the distinction between the core subjects and the others; the latter, with inadequate time initially, are squeezed further by the concentration of time spent upon the former, arising from the end of Key Stage assessment arrangements. For conscientious teachers, the impossibility of resolving the dilemma helps explain why their work is characterised not only by long hours but also by stress and a reduced sense of achievement. (Campbell and Neill, 1992, pp. 62–3)

At Key Stage 2 , similar evidence was collected for the Association of Teachers and Lecturers (ATL) by Webb (1993) although, unlike Campbell's and Neill's studies at Key Stage 1, no systematic surveys were carried out. Instead, 39 schools from 13 LEAs were visited. During these visits, Key Stage 2 teachers and the headteachers were interviewed and one of the teacher's lessons was observed. Data collected from another 11 schools which were part of a different project were included in the final analysis. Of this enlarged sample, 18 per cent consisted of small schools with less than 100 pupils.

These case studies showed that topic work was the main planning approach for delivering Key Stage 2. Most teachers continued with existing projects and subjected them to an analysis to see which programmes of study and attainment targets were covered. Wherever gaps were identified, either new topics were created or the subject was taught as a 'one-off'. In all the schools, mathematics and some aspects of English were taught separately (as was music, some art and PE) although, at the time of the case studies, the orders for these latter subjects were only just published and schools had not had an opportunity to revise their policies. Most teachers when interviewed said that it was impossible to teach all of the National Curriculum in its current form. The majority of the sample gave priority to the core subjects 'whilst interweaving some History, Geography, etc. when we feel that we can do it' (Webb, 1993, p.23).

Two schools among the enlarged sample of 50 (one a 9–13 middle school) had devised a system in which more than half the National Curriculum subjects were taught by subject specialists. It was claimed that this strategy made it easier to determine the patterns of progression within each subject and that specialist teachers could make their class-room a resource centre for their subject. Since work from the different classes was displayed in this resource centre, children could see what other pupils were doing throughout the whole of the school. Assessment of individual progress was also felt to be more easily managed. There were, however, some problems. At first the schools found it difficult to get the balance right between the time required for specialist work and the time that pupils needed to spend with their class teacher. Costs of resources were also appreciably greater when all pupils in the class were doing the same task simultaneously. Many staff expressed concern that they no longer enjoyed an opportunity to develop their expertise in areas outside their specialism.

As with the Key Stage 1 surveys, class size was seen to be a critical limitation to the teacher's ability to deliver the National Curriculum. The average class size in Webb's study was 26. Webb (1993, p.35) argued that, because a commitment to reduce class size is such an important factor when parents consider the choice of a school, head-teachers and governors will continue to resist attempts to modify the class teacher system. This prevents schools from conducting experi-ments to discover whether the use of different staffing structures makes it possible to deliver the National Curriculum more effectively. Webb illustrates this point with the case of a deputy headteacher who was used as a 'floater' to support other junior colleagues in technology. Part of this teacher's time was spent withdrawing groups of pupils (in some cases up to half the class), and the other part in team teaching to improve the knowledge of colleagues. Although this system was felt to work well, the pressure to have smaller classes led to this deputy head being given his own class in the following year, with the result that the flexible arrangements for teaching technology were abandoned.

Pedagogy and the National Curriculum

Webb, in her observations, also attempted to throw some light on the use of different class and organization strategies. Here, however, it is difficult to make direct comparison with the earlier extensive observa-tional research summarized in the previous chapter. In her report Webb (1993) claims that there has been a shift to whole-class teaching as a

result of the National Curriculum and in accordance with the recommendations subsequently endorsed by the National Curriculum Council
(NCC, 1993). Webb's findings show that around 18.5 per cent of the
time was spent in whole-class discussion involving activities such as
teacher demonstration, teacher questioning, etc.; 31.5 per cent of the
time was given over to what Webb described as whole-class teaching,
where an introductory input of about 15 to 20 minutes took place before
pupils were set the same or similar related tasks (what American
researchers such as Brophy and Good [1986] call 'seat work'); 7.4 per
cent of the remaining instructional time was given to cooperative group
work.

In previous observation studies, however, the organization strategy
has been defined in terms of the *audience* and not in terms of the *task
arrangement*. Thus figures of around 66 per cent for individual work in
these studies were obtained during lessons where, for example, the
teacher introduced a new mathematics topic and then circulated around
the classroom interacting with individual children as they answered the
questions in their workbooks. In Webb's analysis, the whole of this
activity would be categorized as a class lesson. However, by making the
assumption that most of the lessons observed by Webb lasted for around
an hour, it is possible to adjust her figures to the same base as the earlier
studies.

According to Webb, most of these 'seat work' lessons contained an
introduction and a concluding period in which the teacher interacted
with the whole class. These periods occupied between 15 and 20
minutes (on average 27 per cent of the hour). Of the 35 per cent of all
instructional time occupied by such lessons, only approximately 9 per
cent would, therefore, have been directed at the whole class (35 per cent
x 27 per cent). If this figure is added to the 18.5 per cent which teachers
used for demonstrations and class discussions, the overall total for class
teaching was around 27 per cent. This result is only a few per cent
higher than the maximum figures obtained in previous observational
studies. For example, Mortimore *et al.* (1988, p.82) give figures of 23
per cent in the second year of junior school and 24 per cent in the third
year for whole-class interactions. Even allowing for the uncertainties
involved in this calculation, it would appear, overall, that there have
been only modest changes in the pattern of organization and interactions used within the junior classroom since the introduction of the
National Curriculum.

This conclusion is supported by the research in small, mostly rural,
primary schools. These have been the subject of continuous study over
the past decade. For example, in the Rural Schools Curriculum

Enhancement National Evaluation (SCENE) Project, carried out for the Department of Education and Science, schools from 14 local authorities were studied (Galton *et al.,* 1991). All the LEAs received an educational support grant specifically to enhance the curriculum in their small rural primary schools. The data collecting period for the SCENE evaluation coincided with Campbell and Neill's first and second surveys when schools were planning for the National Curriculum and were introducing it initially at Key Stage 1. In these small schools (less than 100 pupils with a 5–11 age range), very little change in the patterns of classroom organization was observed, compared to the PRISMS Project (Galton and Patrick, 1990) which was carried out between 1982 and 1986. There were, however, dramatic changes in curriculum coverage and in the amounts of time given to different subjects. Where slight increases in whole-class teaching did occur, these tended to come about in the SCENE project because of the introduction of new subjects where teachers demonstrated to the whole class rather than allowing pupils to engage in self-directed enquiry within collaborative groups. In responding to the question, 'Have any of the curriculum changes caused you to rethink the way you teach?', no teacher in the SCENE sample reported that they had done much more than 'bolt on' the new curriculum demands to their existing practice. Similar issues are being examined in the current follow-up study at Leicester. The focus of this project is the Implementation of the National Curriculum within Small Schools (INCSS). The preliminary findings of the INCSS project confirm OFSTED's (1993a) conclusion that planning procedures have greatly improved as a result of the changes but that the evidence concerning practice is far more 'patchy'.

The Politics of the National Curriculum

During the period when this evidence on curriculum change was being collected, there was also considerable political change, culminating in the removal of Margaret Thatcher as Prime Minister. A brief period of conciliation by Kenneth Baker's successor at the DES, John McGregor, was followed once more by more direct confrontation with the teachers' representatives. Kenneth Clarke's arrival at the DES in November 1990, immediately following his battles at the Department of Health with doctors, ambulance men, nurses and ancillary workers, heralded the eventual demise of Duncan Graham at the NCC and his counterpart at SEAC, Philip Halsey. The chair and the executive position of both bodies were now separated and David Pascal appointed to chair the National Curriculum Council. According to Watkins (1993), however, he was under much closer control of the newly appointed Council members, most of whom had figured strongly as supporters of the 'New Right' movement during the 1980s. Both the new NCC and the SEAC chairs then proceeded to appoint two 'low profile Chief Executives' who were prepared to 'work with increasingly right wing Councils' (Watkins, 1993, p.66). The subject committees were dismantled and, despite the increased political control of appointments, ministers still continued to interfere with the structure and detail of every National Curriculum subject, notably in the revised orders for the English curriculum and the history syllabus at Key Stage 4.

Given this increased political control, it was necessary to find explanations (and scapegoats) to account for the failure of the National Curriculum to bring about the desired changes in primary practice, in particular a greater emphasis on whole-class specialist teaching. Initially, the NCC had recommended that schools should continue to teach topic-based activities since it would be 'counter-productive to lose existing good practice and unhelpful for learning to devise an unnecessary fragmented curriculum' (NCC, 1989, p.7). Now, however, in their advice to the Secretary of State for Education, the Council was in no doubt that 'some of the problems encountered by schools in managing their curriculum are rooted in an adherence to pre-National Curriculum approaches to curriculum organisation and methodology' (NCC, 1993, p.12). As a result, the NCC now recommended 'that serious and urgent attention should be given to the greater use of single subject teaching and of subject teachers' (NCC, 1993, p.13). HMI, reporting on progress in the National Curriculum under the title, *Curriculum Organisation and Classroom Practice in Primary Schools* (OFSTED, 1993a), although attempting to steer a more 'conservative' course, also noticed that there was a shift towards designing topics which were focused on a single subject, but that where there was an unsatisfactory balance between single-subject teaching and topic work, 'it usually erred in the direction of an over-reliance on topics' (p.8). During this period, therefore, a view began to emerge, among those with a vested interest in espousing the cause of the National Curriculum, that while the overall assumptions behind the development of the various programmes of study remained valid, these could not be delivered within thematic or topic approaches since the latter were too closely associated with the old primary ideology. Having reached this conclusion, the Council then set out to find the evidence to support this view.

Given the government's general suspicion of all things educational, its supporters on the reformed National Curriculum Council apparently saw no reason to abandon the original strategy aimed at shifting primary practice towards traditional methods through an emphasis on subject specialism and precise definition of attainment targets. When the evidence clearly showed that this strategy was not working and that teachers were highly resistant to these attempts to change their practice, preferring instead to 'bolt on' the new subject content to their existing pedagogy, the focus of attention shifted. Failure to bring about changes in practice was now attributed to another of the supposed characteristics of progressivism, namely the use of integrated subject teaching. This view was persistently paraded despite the careful analysis of research studies showing that the integrated day, for the most part, existed in theory rather than practice (Alexander, 1992; Simon, 1981a). Scapegoats for this supposed state of affairs were also readily available: it was the local authority's insistence on maintaining these undesirable features as part of 'good primary practice', along with the reactionary views of those responsible for initial teacher training who were blamed for this reluctance by teachers to modify their teaching. In these views ministers were reinforced by the publication of findings of the PRINDEP Project which evaluated Leeds City Council's attempt to improve the quality of provision in its inner-city schools at the cost of some £13 million (Alexander, 1991). (This study will be the subject of detailed discussion in Chapter 4.) It led to the setting up of an enquiry by Kenneth Clarke and the production of what came to be known as 'The Three Wise Men's' Report (Alexander *et al.*, 1992). These 'wise men' questioned the effectiveness of the existing elementary tradition of a single class, generalist primary teacher and recommended instead the use of more class teaching and of more specialist teachers.

During the subsequent debate, few questioned the wisdom of this advice or the evidence on which it was based. Most headteachers attending HMI conferences to discuss 'The Three Wise Men's' Report stressed the importance of improving their teachers' 'subject knowledge' if greater emphasis were to be placed on specialist teaching at Key Stage 2 (OFSTED, 1993a). Research carried out at Exeter appeared to confirm this need. Bennett and Carré (1993) and their team assessed the knowledge required for satisfactorily teaching the first six levels of the National Curriculum science, mathematics and English syllabuses. They reported that postgraduate students' 'substantive and syntactic' knowledge of science was limited. Most students did not have a bank of scientific concepts which they could use to make sense of every day phenomena. Similarly, few students had any understanding of the process of mathematical thinking. Not surprisingly, therefore, they tended to teach routine procedures rather than to teach for understanding when in the classroom. Similar findings have emerged from studies in the United States (Borko and Livingston, 1989).

In language there were clearly established weaknesses in the students' knowledge about the structures of language, especially grammar. Elsewhere, science has been singled out for special attention given that in recent surveys (Bennett et al., 1992; Wragg et al., 1989), the majority of experienced teachers felt competent to teach the National Curriculum without further help or training in only two core subjects: English and mathematics. Attempts have, therefore, been made to improve teachers' conceptual knowledge of science (Summers et al., 1993). These researchers carried out a two-year longitudinal study following the development in 53 primary school teachers' understanding of the concepts of force and energy, two Key Stage 2 National Curriculum programmes of study. Teachers were given short bursts of in-service training, in some cases by science experts and in other cases by school science coordinators. The researchers found that some concepts were more easily understood than others and that there was a gap between the teachers' perception of change in their understanding and the objective assessment of this change (i.e. teachers thought they knew more than they did). The result was a tendency among teachers to develop new misconceptions as a result of the training. Summers et al. (1993) concluded that there was a need to find ways of continuing to support teachers following this training so that their increased understanding would be reinforced and validated. Much the same was said of INSET procedures in general by Bruce Joyce and his colleagues some ten years earlier (Joyce and Showers, 1983).

By the beginning of 1993, therefore, there was a growing body of research evidence that the National Curriculum, as it was originally conceived, was unmanageable. The decision to allow each subject panel to design a 'broad and balanced curriculum', without the availability of any responsible body to oversee its collective impact on the primary school, had resulted in a crisis situation. Typically, a secondary curriculum is planned in terms of its 'logical contingency' (Stake, 1967); in physics, for example, the concept of pressure develops from an understanding of forces. On the other hand, primary teachers tend to build up their pupils' knowledge base by linking it to the pupils' experiences. Reconciling these different approaches to curriculum planning has proved to be difficult. Thomas (1993, p.16) illustrates this point with the geography attainment Target 1, Level 4 (use of four-figure coordinates) by noting that in the 70 years in which he has travelled about, mostly by car, he can only twice remember finding it helpful to use a six-figure map reference!

The crisis in the primary curriculum – the result of this subject matter overload – has been further exacerbated by the inordinately long time required to administer the SATs (Standard Assessment Tasks); this issue will be dealt with more fully in the next chapter. Furthermore, both Webb (1993) and Sammons *et al.* (1994) reported that many of the assessments were found by teachers to be unreliable and that teachers also questioned their validity. The large number of pupils who scored within the Level 2 band has meant that the assessment has lacked the capacity to discriminate effectively. Many teachers have argued, therefore, that the same crude differentiation could be achieved by the use of more rapid impressionistic teacher assessments. When, following the decision of secondary teachers not to carry out the Key Stage 3 assessment programme, primary teachers also refused to carry out the Standard Assessments, it became clear that radical action was needed. The NCC and SEAC were amalgamated and brought back to London where they could be under the close scrutiny of the renamed Department for Education (DfE). Somewhat surprisingly, since the then chair of the NCC, David Pascal, was expected to retain his job, the post was given to Sir Ron Dearing, a noted conciliator and someone with a reputation for being 'a safe pair of hands'. Dearing's initial task was to get the then Minister, John Patten, 'off the hook' in his confrontation with teachers while at the same time preserving the main points of the government's strategy. Accordingly, an intensive round of consultations was undertaken resulting in an Interim Report (Dearing, 1993a), where numerous hints were given that the workload involved in the National Curriculum would be reduced and that the scheme of assessment would be overhauled. Four months later, the Final Report (Dearing, 1993b) was published and sent out for further consultation.

1994: The Dearing Report and the Consultations

Any consideration of both the Interim and Final Dearing reports must recognize that they are essentially political and not educational documents. A crucial factor in the appointment of Sir Ron Dearing, in preference to the favoured candidate of the right-wing of the Conservative party, David Pascal, was the increasing hostility to government policy of the National Association of Headteachers (NAHT), a more 'conservative' association than its rival Secondary Heads Association (SHA). NAHT and its secretary, David Hart, had initially strongly endorsed the National Curriculum, particularly the attempts to bring primary schools 'into line' on the issue of continuity. But the attempted reform of the curriculum, particularly English and history at Key Stages 3 and 4, and John Patten's determination to force through a testing programme at

Key Stage 3 which did not link with the GCSE, was not well received by secondary teachers. Furthermore, this more 'militant' opposition had also encouraged primary colleagues to challenge the government. Dearing's task was, therefore, to end this confrontation, not to conduct an inquest on the government's educational strategy. Thus both the Interim and Final Reports begin by endorsing the existing purposes and structure of the National Curriculum:

> The National Curriculum and its assessment arrangements were introduced as the key initiative in the drive to raise standards. I am clear that these policy initiatives were *well conceived* and are beginning to produce results. (Dearing, 1993a, p.1, emphasis added)

Elsewhere, in Dearing (1993b, p.7), it is again stated that 'the National Curriculum is *fundamental* to raising educational standards'.

Evidence in support of these statements is said to come from the Office for Standards in Education (OFSTED). The research presented in the previous sections, which reached a more modest conclusion, was not cited (Webb, 1993). The findings on the impact of the National Curriculum on teaching and learning, a vital element of improved standards, were even more pessimistic. The largest examination of the impact of the National Curriculum, the Primary Assessment Curriculum and Experience (PACE) project (Pollard *et al.*, 1993; Sammons *et al.*, 1994), provided evidence in its Interim Reports that little had changed within the primary classroom. For example, percentages of time on task were of the same order as those in the earlier observational studies of the 1980s. Similarly, collaborative group work in junior classrooms continued to be a 'neglected art' (Galton, 1981). Although at Key Stage 1 (in comparison to the only other observation study available – Tizard *et al.*, [1988]), there was more pupil teacher interaction in whole-class settings, the Tizard study was unusual in that it deliberately chose classes where there were high proportions of children whose first language was not English. Such children clearly need higher proportions of individual attention. Summing up the position at Key Stage 2, the PACE researchers' stated that:

> In summary, research findings do not suggest that the learning experience for children has become more positive since the introduction of the National Curriculum but it does seem that certain pre-requisites for learning are more in evidence. Teachers have generally acknowledged the benefits of the framework that the National Curriculum provides for the structure of content for planning and teaching ... overall the context for learning has changed since the Education Reform Act. Teacher control in classes has increased, and there is a reduction of opportunity for children to chose and

pace their work. The extent to which the greater teacher control that is needed to organise and manage classrooms in which the National Curriculum is taught is a positive outcome is debatable. (Sammons *et al.,* 1994, p. 64)

Such an analysis hardly justifies the strong endorsement of the National Curriculum found in both of Dearing's reports. Neither is the OFSTED (1993b) evidence, on which the endorsement is said to be based, wholly supportive. The inspectors' survey, based on the examination of 400 lessons in 74 primary schools, indicated there had been little change in classroom practice. Thus 'most teachers did not rule out the value of whole-class teaching but many did not sufficiently exploit the opportunity it provides' (para 11). Furthermore, 'in most of the schools the balanced relationship between whole-class teaching, group work and individual work were not as productive as they should have been resulting in cases of ineffective use of valuable teaching time' (para 12). Thus the general evidence, in so far as it was available to Dearing, should have led to the conclusion that, although planning and progression within subjects had improved as a result of the reforms, six years after the introduction of the National Curriculum teachers were still using a 'bolt on' model whereby new content was adapted to fit existing practice. The discussion in both Dearing reports, however, does not focus upon this crucial issue but concentrates instead on reductions in content and problems of manageability.

This is not to deny the importance of these matters but their emphasis has tended to disguise the fact that the government's policy remained unchanged: to have primary teachers use methods more commonly associated with single-subject secondary teaching with greater use of banding and even streaming. The belief appeared to persist, therefore, that once teachers' legitimate complaints about the excessive demands of the programme were dealt with, the original logic behind the framework for the primary curriculum would produce the desired changes in practice.

Thus one of key recommendations, to slim down the orders, not only to make them less prescriptive but, 'to free some twenty per cent of the teaching time for use at the discretion of the school' (para 4.29), can also be seen as an inducement towards this goal. According to Dearing (1993b) this 20 per cent of allocated time should be viewed as a way of allowing teachers' scope 'to decide how best to motivate pupils in these key years' (para 4.29). This seems a strange rationale since it implies that it may, in future, be difficult to motivate pupils in the core subjects. Presumably during this '20 per cent time', teachers could be expected to operate in ways they had come to believe were important for pupils' learning at this age. It might be hoped, therefore, that primary teachers would be more amenable to 'streamlining' the procedures for teaching the core curriculum to ensure that the time given to the latter did not impinge on the time when they were free to teach in the "old ways'. Once this strategy is understood, then the reasons behind the other main recommendations – the reduction in curriculum content to be *concentrated outside the 'core subjects'* (para 4.3) and the retention, whilst promising to simplify, the ten-level scale (paras 726–7) – fall into place. Although, therefore, the final Dearing report still argues that the National Curriculum at Key Stages 1 and 2 should embrace the concept of entitlement across the whole curriculum, in practice there would seem to be tacit acceptance that what mattered most was to change the way in which English, mathematics and science would be taught in future.

As a way of maintaining the pressure on teachers to change practice within the core areas, the ten-level assessment scale was retained (para 7.60) although there was the promise that steps would be taken to simplify it by reducing the number of attainment targets at both Key Stage 1 and 2 (para 7.27). National Curriculum subjects were to be reviewed (para 4.49) in time for implementation in 1995. Following this review, no further changes would be made for five years (para 4.54). Nowhere in the Final Report is the issue of cross-curriculum themes mentioned, apart from discussing the question of vocational qualifications at Key Stage 4. However, presumably, schools would be free to teach about citizenship, health, the environment and the world of work during the '20 per cent time'.

In summary, therefore, the Dearing Report's recommendations solved the immediate problems associated with the initial form of the National Curriculum and its corresponding assessment procedures, by reducing the content to be covered and by simplifying the attainment targets. However, the fundamental weaknesses which were inherent in the original design were largely ignored. In the end, as Golby (1994, p.102) argues, Dearing's final recommendation that there should be no more change for five years is 'surely a triumph of hope over experience'. The structure of most of the Advisory Groups is a delicate balance between representatives, government nominees from the right and teachers representing the various professional associations. Golby argues that it is doubtful whether any set of recommendations will be able to 'satisfy competing interests while politicians will 'continue to want to earn their reputation through legislative vigour rather than a period of silence; more importantly, there will be new and genuine priorities'. For these reasons, Golby argues that although there are unlikely to be dramatic changes, there will be continuous tinkering. However, if the present changes do not have the desired effect on existing classroom organization and pedagogy, there must be some doubt whether the politicians will be prepared to leave things to develop in the way Golby predicts.

The Future of the National Curriculum Debate

If, however, Golby is correct in his view, then it could mean that primary teachers, either through weariness or disillusion, have allowed a two-tier curriculum to develop with different pedagogies for the core and 20 per cent subjects. Indeed in his last speech before his dismissal, John Patten was reported to have called for a return to streaming in the junior school (*The Independent*, 18 July 1994, p.2). His successor, Gillian Shepherd, the fifth Secretary of State for Education since the introduction of the National Curriculum, may appear to be less ideologically motivated but the government policies set out in this chapter have not changed. Far from accepting a moratorium on debate and leaving the National Curriculum to 'bed down' over the next five years, the case for teachers continuing to challenge the existing rationale on which these reforms were based is perhaps even stronger, given the neglect by Dearing of certain key issues.

The first issue requiring further debate is the concept of *entitlement*. As described in the first chapter, this was originally put forward by curriculum reconstructionalists, such as Denis Lawton, during the 1970s. Entitlement was seen as the right of every pupil to experience a sample of the total culture (where culture represented 'a whole way of life' of a society). The culture represented by the National Curriculum, however, is more akin to Matthew Arnold's earlier use of the word with the emphasis on the subject disciplines and a sharp division between the academic and the vocational. Although, when Lawton first defined key areas of his curriculum his list was not unlike the list of subjects taught in the old grammar school, an important difference concerned the way these areas of human experience were to be organized. Lawton's curriculum would, for example, emphasize citizenship but leave teachers to determine, in light of their pupils' abilities and needs, just how much conventional subject matter should be incorporated within this broad theme. Prior to the introduction of the National Curriculum, secondary schools were beginning to experiment in ways of balancing the demands of entitlement with the needs of individual pupils by introducing modular structures with core and options (Warwick, 1987). This allowed all pupils to receive a minimum entitlement while allowing others to pursue their interests in greater depth. All this experimentation ended, however, once *entitlement* became identified with HMI's notion of a *broad* and *balanced* curriculum and this was perceived as analogous to dietary requirements in which the percentages of fibre (subject A) and fat (subject B) were carefully regulated. How to provide this broad base, while at the same time allowing a pupil to pursue 'excellence' within the context of a National Curriculum, is a dilemma which urgently needs to be resolved.

The second issue which remains largely neglected within both Dearing reports concerns what Campbell (1993) describes as the culture of primary schooling, particularly as it relates to grouping practices. There is ample evidence from the surveys and interviews carried out by both Campbell and Neill (1992) and by Webb (1993) that detailing what must be taught, and indicating how this will be assessed, threatens this culture. For example, Webb (1993, pp.44–5) confirmed that most of the schools with mixed-age classes continued with the usual practice of dividing into age groups within which pupils sat in friendship groups. Only in mathematics were most children grouped by ability. Even here, however, according to Webb, most children only sat and worked together in such ability groups 'when they were given specific individual cooperative group tasks or the teacher taught them as a distinct group'. In an example quoted by Webb (1993, p.45), a teacher had one pupil on Level 6 or 7 in top year mathematics and it was 'hard to keep him going in a class of thirty-four, because he becomes bored quickly'. Some pupils were, therefore, selected to form a small group and, for an hour a day for four days, mathematics was taught in these sets but for the fifth day the teachers took their own classes. During this non-set period, teachers filled in the record of what each pupil had done during the previous week. Attempts to extend this practice to other subjects proved difficult because setting required all classes involved to have a shared timetable and this created problems in the teaching of other subjects where greater flexibility in the use of resources was required.

However, in this school many of its teachers had doubts about this procedure. The deputy head reported that,

> for the very bright pupil it worked, for the least able it partly worked, but I don't think it did anything for the middle group at all. When I started here and was given the top year D Remedial class, you know, of twenty, and I see them now as thirty year olds, holding down responsible jobs and so on. They weren't remedial children, they shouldn't have been stigmatised as such. (Webb, 1993, p.45)

Webb found no teachers who supported streaming. If the only efficient way of delivering the National Curriculum is to increase the requirement to differentiate between pupils then, given the strength of feeling against such grouping practices, teachers will continue to 'graft' the programmes of study onto their existing pedagogy to create a hybridized version. This will prevent necessary progress in those areas of current pedagogy which the research, summarized in Chapter 1, demonstrated requires urgent attention.

Finally, the present structure and organization of the National Curriculum, unchallenged by Dearing, have implications for the distribution of resources. Massive sums have been put into the GEST programmes with the object of improving the subject knowledge of primary teachers, particularly in science, technology and, more recently, in history and geography. The principal strategy has been to offer courses to school coordinators so that they can pass on the expertise gained to colleagues in schools. Yet, as will be seen later in the book, the role of the coordinator has, in the past, not generally been a successful one (Alexander, 1991; Campbell, 1985). Presumably one by-product of this expenditure is that schools will be able to work out ways 'how best to motivate pupils' (Dearing, 1993b, para 4.29). Prior to 1988, however, the evidence from transfer studies (Galton and Willcocks, 1983; Measor and Woods, 1984) showed that primary schools were succeeding in this particular task quite well. Pupils, when writing essays about their hopes after transfer to the secondary school, appeared keen and well motivated, particularly about subjects where they had, as yet, little experience, such as science. Pupils wrote enthusiastically about the visits they had made in the summer term to look at the secondary school's science laboratories and at the other facilities. Six months later, however, the majority of pupils were disillusioned by their experiences and with good reason! Delamont and Galton (1984) 'shadowed' these transfer pupils for a day and found most received a boring diet consisting mainly of copying from books, completing worksheets and drawing diagrams of apparatus, such as a Bunsen burner. Given that a limited amount of money is available for retraining teachers, it would seem preferable to spend it in the lower half of the secondary school where the need appears to be greatest. The present National Curriculum, with its overwhelming emphasis on subject content, must continue to dictate that resources will be directed at primary teachers who are assumed to lack the necessary subject expertise to deliver this curriculum adequately. There may be better ways of spending the money.

The National Curriculum: A Framework or Straitjacket?

In the present political climate, to argue for a National Curriculum which was built around curriculum theory and made modifications in the light of research evidence would seem Utopian. However, there are several countries in continental Europe, such as The Netherlands, where curriculum development takes place within this framework. The pupils appear to do well as a result. For example, in recent international evaluation studies, Dutch primary children were in the top group for mathematics along with those from Hong Kong and Japan. Those responsible for developing the Dutch National Curriculum have been influenced by the ideas of curriculum theorists, such as Michael Hubermann and Roland Vandenberghe. Vandenberghe's analysis, in particular, not only highlighted the problems associated with 'top-down' curriculum development, such as our own National Curriculum, but also the limitations of school-focused 'bottom-up' innovation. The former fails, as we have seen, because teachers are not sufficiently involved in the curriculum decision making and as a result 'bolt on' the new subjects to their existing practice; the formal requirements change but the practice does not. But 'bottom-up' alternatives, although they may initially produce radical change, also lead to stagnation. Schools become committed to the initial 'hard won' changes and are suspicious of any new initiative, even when it appears to be in the national interest (Vandenberghe, 1984).

Vandenberghe, therefore, recommends a combination of both approaches in which the local authority adviser pays a key role in transmitting the anxieties and problems of implementation at school level to those responsible for policy making, and equally transmits to schools the political, social and economic factors which require policy makers to change the existing educational system. In The Netherlands, having set out the framework for the National Curriculum in 1975 – a framework very similar to our own – a number of 'experimental' schools were given the task of making this framework a practical reality (Van Den Brink and Van Bruggen, 1990). Schools were given additional funding for staff and resources on the strict understanding that by the end of the experimental period the programme would be working within normal funding levels. These experimental or 'mother schools' then acted as support schools when others began to develop their own versions of the National Curriculum. Another difference from our own scheme was the time-scale of the reform. The Act implementing the National Curriculum was not passed until 1983, some eight years after the discussions setting up the experiment were commenced (CDCC,

1987). Something of the flavour of the approach can be seen in the document supplied by The Netherlands' Ministry of Education and Science to parents, with the title, *Going to School in The Netherlands.* Under the section 'Textbooks and Teaching', it is explained to parents that:

> Every primary school in The Netherlands has a school curriculum which contains details of precisely what pupils have to learn and the books to be used. The school draws up its own curriculum. The subjects a school is obliged to teach are laid down by law but the manner chosen and the books used are decided by the school itself. The curriculum is inspected by the Government.

In 1993, the first cohort of children who begun their education under the new Act transferred to secondary school. During their period of primary education, following the Primary Education Act of 1985, five further orders in Council have been issued. To assess the effect of these changes, the Ministry of Education commissioned a series of research studies and evaluations to coincide with the first full cycle of the new style primary education. These results were presented to an international audience in September 1993, prior to final presentation to the Ministry for action under the title *Primary Education in The Netherlands, Context, Curricula, Processes and Results.* The evaluation report identifies excessive class size and mixed-age classes as major problems, as well as the overloading of the curriculum with what are termed 'factual subjects'. It also notes the poor quality of many teaching materials and that even after nearly ten years of reform, 'teachers' classroom strategy' is still not sufficiently oriented towards differentiated teaching and catering to the needs of individual children. The researchers point out that,

> all too often teachers are still differentiating in terms of the pace at which children work, even though it is now clear that weaker pupils lose out with this approach, or in terms of levels of attainment, an approach shown by research seldom to produce any perceptible effect.

Unlike the National Curriculum Council's or OFSTED's advice, however, this document sets out in very clear terms a number of desirable changes in teaching strategies. For example, it suggests situations where it is appropriate to use what it terms the 'BHV model' (direct instruction). Basic material is taught through demonstration (B), then practised (H), allowing competency to be mastered in a variety of ways. It is then developed by the use of in-depth material (V) closely tailored to the capacities of individual pupils (CEB, 1993). As a result of this evaluation, the Government has decided to set clearer attainment targets linked to objectives which, unlike those in the UK, will be expressed as the time typically required to achieve a given performance level. Special in-service programmes carrying additional qualifications are being developed. Because university courses are thought too academic for primary teachers, the Ministry of Education has instituted its own National Diploma which it has franchised to colleges and to Pedagogic Centres. These changes have met very little resistance from schools or the professional organizations.

It may not be too late to think along these lines during the Dearing five-year moratorium. Rather than continue with the present system of Advisory Committees followed by superficial consultation exercises, certain schools could be resourced to tackle the key issues identified in this chapter within the agreed National Curriculum framework. However, successful implementation requires two further preconditions. First, there is a need both by policy makers and teachers for a better understanding of the factors that inhibit or promote curriculum change at classroom level. These matters will be discussed in Chapters 5 and 6. Second, a review of the assessment methodology within the National Curriculum is urgently required so that the statements of attainment are no longer seen as a means to engineer curriculum change. One characteristic of the Dutch system is that it clearly distinguishes the assessment procedures used in schools to determine the effectiveness of what is termed 'customized teaching' (i.e. the arrangements to ensure adequate differentiation and progression) from those used to determine national standards and to compare Dutch pupils with children from other countries. In the United Kingdom, however, it is argued that these two functions, the diagnostic and the measurement of national standards, can both be determined from the same assessment measure of attainment. Just why this view has prevailed and its implications for classroom practice will be explored in the next chapter.

Chapter 3
The Mess that is Assessment

Nobody, certainly not after the events at the beginning of 1993, can be in any doubt that the current situation concerning the assessment of children at Key Stages 1 and 2 has reached a point where, if it were politically possible, it would be better to abandon the present programme and start again. Buoyed up by the success of their secondary colleagues in resisting the introduction of tests for 14-year-olds, primary teachers at last expressed their dissatisfaction and in the Spring of 1993 voted to put a temporary halt to testing.

Government spokespersons have portrayed this resistance as yet another example of the prevailing ideology within a teaching profession that is indifferent to its attempts to raise national standards. The two main teacher unions, while accepting the need for assessment, have seemed to imply that its sole purpose was to provide teachers with diagnostic information. Even so, concerns have been expressed about the value of some of the testing instruments, in that they do not produce results which differ substantially from the judgements that teachers make, during the course of the year, based on frequent observation of their pupils. At Key Stage 1, for example, the time required to test a class of pupils can occupy several weeks of the summer term (Campbell and Neill, 1992). However, attempts at Key Stage 2 to improve the situation by using, whenever possible, a group test, based on the use of pencil and paper measures, has raised protests from teacher representatives who see this move as a way of restoring the former 11-plus examination. Those involved in the reform of the assessment procedures therefore find themselves in a 'catch 22' situation in which, apart from reducing the number of attainment levels to cut down on the length of time required to administer the practical tasks, there is little that can be done at the present time which will satisfy all parties involved in the assessment process.

Any discussion about the present confusion must begin with the document which initiated the debate, the TGAT (1988) report. The report made a number of assumptions about the nature of the assessment process, the chief one being (paras 23–7) that it was possible to design a procedure which would both monitor national standards and enable teachers to diagnose pupils' learning difficulties. This claim was partly based on the experience acquired by several members of the committee who were previously involved in the APU (Assessment and Performance Unit). Indeed, despite the problems which have arisen over the introduction of the Standard Assessment Tasks, it appears that even the research community is now willing to look back on the operation of the APU as a time when radical progress was made in developing new techniques for assessing pupil's progress. BERA's (British Educational Research Association) Policy Task Group on Assessment has, for example, recommended that a bank of assessment procedures and test items be created (with existing APU and some early pilot SATs materials providing a substantial start). The bank would be used as a resource for teachers to supplement or check their own assessment of individual pupils, for surveys of national performance involving only a light sample of pupils, and as a means to feedback to teachers the national performance on specific aims to help in the interpretation of the performance of their own pupils (Harlen *et al.,* 1992, p.216).

Very few voices have been raised against these proposals, an important exception being Professor Harvey Goldstein who has from the outset been a critic of the APU approach. He argues that it is not possible to have 'an open choice item bank which also conveys unbiased information on national performance levels whether for feedback to teachers or for incorporation into a national survey' (Goldstein, 1993, p.122). The arguments which lie behind Goldstein's point of view will be developed in this chapter. The mess that is assessment has therefore been created, in part, by attempting to view recent curriculum assessment history in a way which appears to gloss over the grave difficulties encountered during these earlier developments.

The debate has also been marked by a seeming unwillingness on the part of the reformers to consider research evidence concerning different assessment procedures and by the tendency to regard psychometric techniques as wholly inappropriate to the present requirements. As a result, many statements made about the assessment process during recent debates are rarely qualified or challenged. To take an example, it is frequently said that a standardized test tells you nothing about a pupil's progress. But in primary level mathematics, items on standardized tests bear a great similarity to the same practice tasks on which pupils spend a large proportion of their time during lessons. It is not unreasonable to argue that such tests do measure, to some degree, the extent to which pupils have mastered the processes involved in such calculations.

Even when the above proposition is accepted, there are those who fall back on the argument that 'such tests only tell you whether a pupil can recognize the right answer, not whether they understand how to arrive at that answer'. Here again, this seems to be a comment on how such tests are used rather than a denial of their intrinsic worth, since a few minutes of the teacher's time devoted to asking pupils to explain their working goes a long way to meet such negative criticism.

Those who criticize formal testing often argue that primary teachers, because of the time they spend with their pupils, are the best people to make judgements about an individual's performance. Whilst such a statement has a self-evident 'ring of truth', it does not always stand up to empirical investigation. Many studies, notably in this country that by Croll and Moses (1985), have demonstrated that teachers often base their judgements of pupils' performance in specific areas on general notions of ability (usually associated with reading age) or on behavioural factors. Croll and Moses observed pupils who were said to have special learning difficulties and noted those who were engaging in high levels of disruptive behaviour. These pupils invariably received lower ratings in terms of academic performance than other pupils with comparable ability. It may be true, as Gipps et al. (1991) assert, that as a result of the SATs exercise, teachers are becoming better observers of their pupils, although this is directly contradicted by Desforges et al. (1994). But there are certainly no grounds for complacency and no grounds, as some would argue, for using teacher assessments as the major means of judging pupils' performance and national standards.

The purpose of this brief discussion is not to make the case for standardized testing but to urge that decisions about the most appropriate test procedures should be made only after public scrutiny of the available empirical evidence about their effectiveness. Different forms of assessment will serve different purposes and it may be wise, therefore, to begin any discussion by looking at the different approaches to assessment and considering what they have to offer. From there we will look at what is known about the working of the APU and the ways in which its methods have been incorporated uncritically into the present assessment process. Finally, we will examine some data available on the assessment of science pupils, perhaps the most difficult area within the core curriculum, before going on to make some recommendations about future policy.

What Tests are Supposed to Test

It is too often ignored by critics of traditional assessment procedures that their original purpose was to create equal opportunities in advancement, thereby reducing the dangers of nepotism. Early test procedures relied heavily on the candidates' ability to recall information or to solve specific problems based on that information. It was possible to argue that such tests were clearly distinct from the qualities demanded by intelligence tests with their emphasis on abstract reasoning. In the early days of test development, therefore, it was perfectly acceptable to use an intelligence test to predict performance on an attainment test. The same predictive measure (the IQ test) could be used at various intervals to act as a standard against which changes in attainment scores over time could be assessed. In this way, for example, comparisons could be made between the performance of pre-war and post-second world war pupils from rural and urban schools.

In developing these attainment tests, those constructing the instruments were concerned to ensure that the instrument had both reliability and validity. It is fairly common for recent writers, because of the emphasis primarily put on the former measure, to emphasize the need to stress validity, even at the expense of reliability (James and Conner, 1993). In general terms, validity is conceived as indicating that the test measures what it purports to measure, whereas reliability is concerned with the result obtained being consistent. However, these two measures are not mutually exclusive. A result which is reliable is obviously measuring something consistent although that something may not be what the test purports to measure. In that sense, therefore, one can have a test which is reliable but not valid. However, it is difficult to envisage how one can develop a test which is valid but unreliable. For example, if one took a test consisting of 50 short questions, arbitrarily divided into two halves and found that the aggregate score on the two halves of the test did not correspond for the majority of pupils, then a likely conclusion would be that the two halves of the test did not measure the same thing. It is, of course, possible to argue, for example, that when the same test is given on two occasions, it possesses validity but has low reliability because it is affected by the variability of the day-to-day performance of pupils. But it is difficult to know in what sense such validity could have any useful meaning, in that the test has only practical value if it can be shown to give consistent results. This latter point is not purely academic since it has particular implications for any assessment of measures which are performance-based, such as those favoured by the Assessment and Performance Unit. As will be seen later for both the APU measures and to a lesser degree in the development of the SATs, the validity criterion appears at times to be the sole determinant of whether a test item should be used to monitor pupil performance.

The situation is complicated by the fact that ways in which both validity and reliability are determined depend on the nature of the measurement being made. In tests which mainly require pupils to remember information, the most important aspect of validity is *content* validity: whether the chosen questions sampled the entire syllabus and not just a portion of it. If this were not so, then some pupils might do well simply because they were lucky enough to have studied the topics covered by the questions. Intelligence tests, on the other hand, because they are designed to test abstract reasoning, are considered to be largely independent of content. *Construct* validity – whether a group of items adequately represents a particular domain within the model of the intellect used to construct the intelligence test – is now the more important. A complicated mathematical process, known as factor analysis, is mostly used to estimate this type of validity. However, to save time, many test constructors attempt to eliminate suspect items, before piloting the test, by bringing together a group of experts who are asked to place each of the items under what they consider to be the appropriate domain. When items are classified in this way they are said to have *face* validity.

As attainment tests began to make more complex intellectual demands and became not unlike intelligence tests in form, the distinction between content and construct validity tended to disappear. For example, the APU science attainment tests purported to measure various scientific domains such as hypothesizing, observing and inferring. In this context, as Messick (1989) rightly argues, content validity becomes subsumed into construct validity in that if the test does not adequately sample the various demands made upon the pupil during the series of lessons, it will not adequately reflect the domains which the lessons seek to cover. Finally, there is a further form of validity, *predictive* validity, which is less often mentioned. When purporting to test process skills in science, such as the ability to hypothesize, it is reasonable to ask whether the results of such a test do predict future performance in a variety of different contexts. Those who develop APU-style measures of assessment often appear to assume that, because the test situation is 'authentic', in that it attempts to replicate a real classroom activity, it is by definition a satisfactory predictor of future classroom performance in the same domain.

Are Consistent Results Necessary?

Turning to the question of reliability, the measure used again depends on the nature of the test administered. Inconsistency in test results arises because of random errors which can develop from various sources. A pupil's performance may differ from day to day but not in a consistent manner across the class as a whole. Markers may be inconsistent, either when judging the performance of different pupils on a single occasion or when assessing the performance of the same pupil at different times. The effect of the first kind of error would best be established by giving the same test on two separate occasions and determining the average agreement between the scores of all pupils. The second kind of error could be determined by asking several examiners to mark the same set of test papers or observe the same group of children and calculating the inter-observer agreement. On a written test it would be likely that the 'between occasions' reliability would be regarded as the main source of error and given greater prominence. When rating pupils' performance live in the classroom, however, the 'inter-rater reliability' of the judges would be the dominant concern.

Norm-referenced and Criterion-referenced Tests

There is also a third major source of unreliability relating to the composition of the test itself. For example, with a written test consisting of 50 short questions, it would be possible for several pupils to obtain the same total score while answering different combinations of questions on the test paper. We, nevertheless, make the assumption that two pupils with, say, a total score of 25 are of the same standard. This is only true if there is some consistency between the different items.

Early test constructors put most of their effort into ensuring a high degree of internal consistency between each test item because their purpose in testing was to determine an 'individual's performance in relation to that obtained by a typical pupil'. These tests were therefore called *norm-referenced*. When designing such a test it is important to spread the marks of the pupils out as far as possible in order to make certain that they are correctly placed relative to the other candidates. This is best accomplished by varying the difficulty level of the items (percentage of the sample passing) and ensuring that each item positively discriminates in favour of candidates who get the highest total scores. When these conditions are maximized, the test is likely also to have a high degree of internal consistency.

These methods of analysis, however, are inappropriate where the test constructor is not attempting to measure a standard but to assess performance, as proposed by TGAT (1988). Such tests are often called *criterion-referenced* because they determine whether the candidate is capable of meeting a set criterion and the major concern is to ensure that a candidate's score is a reliable estimate of success. To achieve this reliability it is necessary to determine a threshold level of performance, namely the point at which the criterion is either passed or failed, and then construct lots of items which measure this level of performance. Only in this way can one be certain that passing is not a lucky occurrence. Unlike norm-referenced tests, therefore, there should be little variation in the levels of item difficulty and consequently measures of internal consistency are no longer relevant. The most appropriate form of reliability is test-retest.

Although the above discussion may appear somewhat unnecessarily detailed, it has major relevance to the debate about testing as it currently takes place in the United Kingdom. The major purpose of a norm-referenced test is, as we have seen, to determine the *standard* of performance relative to other pupils either on the same or on a previous occasion. The major purpose of the criterion-referenced test is to enable a pupils' *level* of performance to be determined in order that a teacher can, for example, make a diagnosis as to whether it is necessary to re-teach the material. These latter tests were shown to be very effective during World War II in improving the quality of aircraft maintenance. The principles governing the construction of such tests become more difficult to apply, however, when the criterion measure is not the ability to strip down a carburettor but to hypothesize why a particular pattern is displayed by a range of scientific data. For this reason, test constructors have ceased to talk about *criterion-reference* testing in relation to school subjects and prefer instead to talk about such performance tests being *domain-* or *objective-referenced*. Although in practice it is difficult to distinguish between a 'norm-referenced' question and an 'objective-referenced' one, it is the way such items are combined that should determine the use to which the test is put. It should be clear, however, that it is very difficult to design a satisfactory single test which will both estimate differences in standards between pupils and which will also operate as an efficient diagnostic instrument for teachers wishing to determine how best to proceed in matters of instruction. Yet it is these dual demands which the SATs purport to satisfy.

The result, so far, has been the worst of both worlds. Teachers have found that the distinctions between SAT scores of one, two or three are too broad, and open to misinterpretation for effective diagnoses. The scores also fail to discriminate effectively between pupils, making any judgement about standards between schools or between pupils from one year to another uncertain. For teachers, therefore, the work involved to produce such SAT scores seems highly disproportionate in relation to the perceived benefits.

It is important, however, not to proceed from this point to the argument that because the SATs do not give an adequate measure of performance over intervals of time, we should abandon attempts to measure standards. Unless solutions to these problems are found, the sterile debate concerning the merits of different forms of primary education which has continued, as Chapter 1 demonstrated, for over two decades, will remain unresolved. More importantly, it will also be impossible to identify inequalities in the system where, because of inadequate teaching or resourcing, pupils in some schools receive a poorer education than others. Before examining possible solutions to the current difficulties, however, it is first necessary to look at the part played by the APU which, despite the apparent incompatibility between norm- and criterion-referenced testing, decided to opt for a single test capable of satisfying these conflicting demands.

Solving the Assessment Problem: The APU Approach

The first attempt at monitoring national standards came with the setting up of the Assessment and Performance Unit in 1974. The Unit was charged with overseeing and surveying the performance in mathematics and languages at the ages of 11 and 15 and of science at the ages of 11, 13 and 15. The mathematics and language test development was contracted out to the National Foundation for Educational Research (NFER) while Leeds University and Chelsea College, London were responsible for science. Work also took place in assessing the performance of modern languages but for present purposes the discussion will be restricted to what are now the core National Curriculum area subjects. Whatever the rhetoric subsequently surrounding the work of the APU, there can be little doubt that the question of standards was to the forefront at the time of its creation. In 1976 the Unit's first publicity leaflet, setting out its aims, declared that:

> The first task of the APU is to identify and define standards of performance pupils might be expected to achieve throughout their work at school. Next, it has to find generally acceptable ways of measuring and assessing pupils' achievement against these standards to decide at what ages assessment should be done.

Coincidentally with the creation of the APU, advances in test construction were being developed in the United States using a procedure known as Rasch (1966) analysis. It was shown in an earlier section of this chapter that one of the main weaknesses of standardized tests in determining national standards concerned the non-equivalence of candidates' test scores. The Rasch methodology was particularly relevant to this problem in that it claimed to set each item on a unitary scale such that the likelihood of a correct response to any question depended only on two criteria: the candidate's ability and the difficulty of the question. Thus, provided that there were common elements to anchor the measurement scale, then the difficulty of any question could be represented in terms of an absolute ability score such that differences in scores over time were only dependent on the capability of the candidate. Once each question (referred to as an item) was calibrated in terms of its difficulty (expressed in units of ability) different items could be related to each other irrespective of the content tested. The NFER chose to express the unit of ability as a 'wit' and somewhat ironically introduced the notion of a 'half-wit'! For ease of calculation the wit was broken up into 100 smaller units (the centi-wit) and it was claimed after trials undertaken in Israel that the average pupil, typically, gained around 200 centi-wits a year in most subjects.

Using Rasch Analysis thus solves the problem of content validity. It now becomes theoretically possible to create large banks of items covering a wide range of content. Provided that all the items have agreed face validity, namely, a panel of experts have agreed that the items, although measuring different content areas, do test the same ability or skills, a teacher in any school merely selects from this bank of items appropriate questions which mirror the content of his or her lesson. The answers to each question are then scored in centi-wits and aggregated for the particular ability or skill being measured. The results of pupils from one school can also be compared with those of another school, even though each group of pupils may have answered a different set of questions from the item bank. In the same way it is also possible to measure differences in the performance of pupils on the same tests over time. Even if it is felt that cultural change renders some test questions inappropriate at the later date, provided that the old test and the new test partly overlap, it is possible to calibrate the new test items on the same scale as the old ones. Although there were objections at the time to the Rasch approach, particularly to the assumptions that a pupil's response was not affected by the teaching, nor by the exposure to different kinds of curricula, those from the NFER who argued for Rasch did so on the grounds that while it might not be an exact description of educational reality, 'It was nevertheless a useful staring point and did give simple useful summaries of test score data' (Gipps and Goldstein, 1983, p.63).

The APU science group, however, took a different approach to the problem of criterion-referenced measurement. They sought to make use of generalizability theory (Johnson and Bell, 1985). This approach did not rely upon the rather simplistic assumptions of Rasch but hypothesized that, provided that the test items had face validity, then the aggregate score of an individual or of a class was akin to a sample mean which was related in some way to a series of population parameters. Provided that sufficient items were available, so that pupils could achieve their aggregate score using various combinations of items, it was possible to relate these scores to a population ability parameter (in effect to use the less reliable sample score to estimate a true population score).

This method had been first advocated by the National Assessment of Educational Progress (NAPE), the body responsible for coordinating the design of new test procedures in the United States. NAPE, however, was unable to develop a suitable analysis programme, the major problem being that to sample a range of any particular measure satisfactorily demanded an impossibly large number of items. At the time, given the enormous sums that had been spent on the enterprise, it was too damaging politically to abandon the venture and to admit failure. The monitoring exercise was, therefore, continued but the items were now selected, mainly on the basis of their face validity and their difficulty level, using the more familiar techniques originally developed for norm-reference testing. However, within this criterion-referenced framework, as discussed previously, it was no longer possible to use internal consistency coefficients to estimate reliability and the constraints of time and the unwillingness of teachers prevented the use of an alternative procedure such as test-retest correlations. The tests were, therefore, now said to be 'objective referenced'. As such, they represented a rather unsatisfactory psychometric compromise between the norm-referenced and criterion-referenced approaches.

Shortly after the setting up of the APU, its director, together with the director of the NFER, went on a tour of the United States to assimilate lessons from the American experience. Their report (Burstall and Kay, 1978) devoted much space to expressing concerns about the pressure that the American testing programme exerted on teachers and pupils and of the backwash effect on the curriculum. There was very little detailed discussion of the technical difficulties associated with the analysis. Indeed, the authors of the report took an optimistic view that the technical difficulties associated with the construction of the 'new style' tests would soon be solved. In the United Kingdom, progress continued on the development of the new APU tests. Between 1977 and 1980, when two specially convened seminars were held, the NFER became increasingly isolated in its advocacy of the Rasch methodology. According to Gipps and Goldstein (1983), delays in coming to a decision, coupled with strongly critical reactions from the research community, gradually led the APU to hedge its bets and abandon its commitment to this particular analytical approach.

At the same time, the attempts by the science group to use generalizability theory also began to attract criticism from the Advisory Statistics Group within the APU. Members of the group were concerned about the validity of this technique when the universe of items was little more than three times as large as the length of the test finally selected. Perhaps because of the heated arguments generated over the use of the Rasch methodology, the issue of generalizability never received the detailed consideration it merited. In practice, once the pilot tests had been carried out, its use became increasingly problematic. This was because the pupils' performance was shown to be highly task-dependent. There was thus limited generalizability from task to task which therefore brought into question the major assumption of this method, that the different groups of items included in any one test could be considered as samples drawn from a single population.

The importance of this discussion, in relation to National Curriculum testing, is that from around 1980 up to the Educational Reform Act of 1988, no approved statistical measure existed which would enable the results from these APU tests to be compared over time. The original aim of the APU, namely to discover whether standards were falling or rising, could not therefore be achieved. Not surprisingly, as had happened in the United States, the political consequences of such an admission were too great and the exercise was, therefore, continued using a similar strategy to that employed by the American NAPE, whereby results were reported separately for each of the items. Having abandoned any notion of grouping items and providing criterion scores, the only measure available to determine the appropriateness of a particular test item was the agreement among judges that it offered face validity, coupled with a demonstration during trials that it did not present too many practical difficulties within the classroom. The original intention of comparing performance over time was largely ignored, other than to offer the suggestion that by using a small number of items on consecutive occasions it might be possible to use the scores to moderate across the two testings. There matters rested and in due course surveys in science, mathematics and language were conducted throughout the period 1980 to 1984.

The analysis of the science tests presented some of the greatest difficulties. By the time the final report (APU, 1989) was published, the word 'standard' no longer appeared in the index. The main purpose of the science survey was now 'to monitor pupils' levels of performance in each of a number of different aspects of science activity' (APU, 1989. p.35). Insofar as comparisons were made across age groups, these were done either by comparing individual questions or by comparing scores on sub-categories of items which, through face validity, were said to represent a given domain. These included, for example, reading information from graphs, tables and charts and planning parts of investigations. In some cases, a specially designed set of questions or 'probes', for use across different age ranges, was developed.

Various difficulties associated with these comparisons are briefly discussed in Chapter 13 of the report where, for example, the extent to which the differences recorded were influenced by the need to select materials accessible to the complete age range is considered. Throughout the reports, little attention is given to the fact that many of the items were shown to be content-dependent, a finding which appears to apply universally to science tests (Linn et al., 1991). For these reasons, the APU science team indicated a preference for comparisons between single items.

Thus, in summary, by the end of the 1980s a position was reached where a team of science experts might decide, for example, that a question about the rate at which a stream of water emerged from a container was a valid measure of the pupils' ability to plan an investigation. This question would be trialled with a sample of pupils and their responses used to develop a marking scheme. Let us suppose around 50 per cent of the population of 11-year-old pupils obtained at least one-third of the allocated marks. If, in future years, more than 50 per cent of 11-year-olds obtained better marks when answering the same question, it would be assumed that, nationally, the ability to plan experiments had improved. At no time during this testing programme is any attempt made to determine whether this question had predictive validity, in the sense that pupils who obtained high scores were observed planning more effective experiments during science lessons. This, then, was the 'state of the art' of assessment at the point where the APU's work and publications were subsumed within the Schools Examination and Assessment Council (SEAC) which, along with the National Curriculum Council (NCC), was chosen to implement the 1988 educational reforms.

SEAC and the Development of the Standard Assessment Tasks

Given the difficulties experienced by the APU teams it may be thought somewhat surprising that the Task Group on Assessment and Testing report should come out so strongly in favour of designing a national assessment system based 'on a combination of moderated teacher ratings and Standard Assessment Tasks' (TGAT, 1988, para 63). Undoubtedly, the political circumstances of the time made such a recommendation inevitable. At the beginning of the renewed debate about the need to assess standards of performance in schools, the then Prime Minister, Margaret Thatcher, went on record in demanding something which was simple, straightforward and *cheap*. The TGAT group. under the chairmanship of Professor Paul Black, were therefore under immense pressure to produce an assessment scheme which, in theory at least, was uncomplicated. Any recommendation to develop a range of different tests to fulfil the different functions required of the national assessment scheme was, therefore, politically unacceptable. During the consultations there was a widespread fear that criticizing the TGAT proposals might open the door to the 11-plus style of pencil and paper tests. Only a few commentators questioned the report's claim that a single test could be used for both accountability and diagnostic purposes.

Of crucial importance, within the TGAT recommendations, was the view that the national assessment system should be based on a combination of moderated teacher ratings and Standard Assessment Tasks (para 63). This was because teacher ratings of themselves were open to misrepresentation, since they were 'strongly influenced by local expectations of achievement'. More importantly, the Standard Assessment Tasks (para 47) were not to be restricted to the written form but could involve practical or oral modes. This, it was claimed, would afford greater curriculum validity, in that by expanding the range of possibilities there was less chance of discontinuity between the teacher's own assessment of everyday classroom activities and the work required for the test. Behind this decision lies, it would appear, an assumption that, because different forms of test carry different sources of unreliability, combinations of measures (using written, oral and practical tests) would produce a more satisfactory estimate of a pupil's ability. This is because the different sources of measurement error would tend to cancel each other out. Another argument used to advocate mixed-mode testing was (para 48) that it increased the ability range of pupils who could be tested, particularly those who experienced problems with the written mode.

The argument against conventional forms of written testing is similar to the one used by Drummond (1993, p.1) who tells of the time that she scrutinized the test booklet of a 7-year-old pupil called Jason. This particular pupil answered one correct question out of 36 and Drummond concludes, as a result of this experience, that questions about testing are not primarily organizational or pedagogical but moral and philosophical, to do with such issues as *why* assess rather than *when* and *how*. This position inevitably leads Drummond towards an assessment policy based upon teacher's observation and diagnosis rather than on the use of pencil and paper tests or, indeed of any kind of procedure that smacks of quantification and standardization.

At least Drummond is consistent in her rejection of objective and mechanical forms of assessment in favour of processes which enable teachers to understand the way that children, such as Jason, seek to learn. The TGAT report, partly, as we have seen, for political reasons, opted for combinations of objective and more impressionistic assessment procedures, notwithstanding that this increased tremendously the assessment load upon both teachers and pupils. The effects of this multiplicity of procedures, particularly the problems of administering the various tests in a fair manner, have become increasingly evident (Cooper, 1992; Gipps, 1992).

Recent evaluations of the SATs seem intent on ignoring these weaknesses. For example, the report on the STAIR consortium pilot study of Key Stage 1 materials (SEAC, 1991, p.30) rules out any 'post hoc' moderation procedures in favour of 'communicating standards in advance'. The report argues, with a certain degree of optimism, that if the tasks selected only relate to a single statement of attainment, there is control of information provided and the extent of teacher prompting is restricted. Both these features should enhance reliability.

Just how far this optimism is misplaced can be see by the report of the PACE (Primary Assessment Curriculum and Experience) project, based at the University of Bristol. These researchers observed the operation of the same standard assessment task in a number of classrooms (Abbott *et al.*, 1994). Although the particular SAT (sinking and floating) has now been dropped from the assessment programme, the authors concluded from their observations of other assessment activities that the problems encountered during the science-based activity were also prevalent in other curriculum areas. To begin with, there were differences in the circumstances in which the SAT was conducted. In one classroom (Medway), the apparatus was set up in a corner of the classroom within easy reach of a sink, while at another (Greenside) the children had to work in a cramped and inconvenient room where water had to be fetched from the cloakroom. Once this SAT equipment had been set up there was little room left on the tables for the children to write. In the third school (Leigh), the conditions were more ideal, with a special area providing two sinks with space to set out tables where children could write up their results in a dry area.

The arrangement of the class also had an effect on the teacher's ability to obtain consistent data. In Medway, for example, the teacher had to cope with the remainder of the class at the same time that she was carrying out the SAT exercise and often had to break off in order to help deal with the demands of other children. At Greenside, however, a classroom ancillary was provided so that the teacher was free to conduct the SAT, while at Leigh the headteacher provided support.

Such variations in conditions clearly affect a teacher's ability to record accurately the performance of the children. However, as Abbott and her colleagues demonstrated, a further element of unreliability was introduced into the assessment exercise because the practice of the three teachers diverged greatly, particularly in the way in which they led children or were ready to accept pupils' answers as evidence of their ability to 'interpret findings' or make 'a generalization'. In almost every case the amount of time available for the child to complete the task also varied. The unreliability of these assessments has been further demonstrated by Shorrocks et al. (1992). Shorrocks and her colleagues were asked to develop a series of probes by SEAC in order to examine the consistency between the teachers' assessments and the SATs. In the specification for the evaluation, SEAC excluded the possibility of any observation study of the kind that the PACE team engaged in. No attempt was made, therefore, to determine predictive validity (whether completing the SATs satisfactorily was an indication that pupils could demonstrate similar skills under normal classroom conditions). There was no way, therefore, of knowing how valid the probes developed by Shorrocks were. All that could be said was that if all three scores – teacher assessments (TA), SATs and probes – were highly correlated then there was a degree of reliability and construct validity in the assessment process.

However, it was found that the scores obtained with these probes were in general lower than either the TA or the SATs score and Shorrocks concluded that the scoring of the SATs and the TAs left something to be desired in terms of 'dependability', 'validity' and 'comparability' (Shorrocks et al., 1992, p.236). Neither do the problems of reliability and validity appear to be associated solely with the science questions, although their interpretation does appear to give rise to more serious concerns. The PACE researchers also visited schools during 1992 when a mathematics SAT was being carried out and their observations suggested that,

This apparently more standardised task was equally vulnerable to variations in the way teachers present the activity: group sizes, the latitude allowed in terms of time, in permitting children to count on fingers for what are meant to be tests of recall and in other ways. It is clear that this type of assessment, too, has its limitations and would not solve all difficulties. (Abbott *et al.*, 1994, p.171)

Clearing up the Mess

The final Dearing Report, *The National Curriculum and its Assessment* (Dearing, 1993b) does not face up to these issues but continues to support a single domain-referenced system for both formative and summative assessment (para 7.11). Much of the argument in the review concerns the retention of the ten-level scale, coupled with the proposal to slim down the number of statements of attainment at Key Stages 1 and 2. The Report concludes that the ten-level scale should be retained but 'fine tuned' by introducing more distinct criteria to produce finer gradings. This was particularly necessary for Level 2, where in mathematics at Key Stage 1, for example, 70 per cent of the pupils achieved competence. The report appears to assume that it will be possible to define these criteria unambiguously in ways which allow teachers to make reliable and valid assessments. The evidence so far collected from the studies by Abbott *et al.* (1994), however, suggests otherwise but the implications of this and other relevant research are not dealt with in the Report.

Among the other evidence is some collected as part of the STAR (Primary Science Teaching Action Research) project carried out jointly by the School of Education, University of Leicester and the Centre for Research in Primary Science and Technology in the Department of Education at the University of Liverpool, from January 1986 to September 1989. The STAR project used three measures to assess performance. The first was a written test not unlike those produced by the APU, the second was a practical task very similar to that used in the Key Stage 1 SAT, and the third measure required observations of the pupils engaged in similar activities during normal lessons. The tests were used to assess pupils' performance in eight distinct domains identified in earlier studies by Harlen (1983), herself a member of the APU science team. Table 3.1 shows the correlations between the pupils' scores on the written and practical exercises.

Table 3.1 Intercorrelations between Key Stage 2 written and practical tasks

Domain	Correlation	Sig. Level
Measuring	0.28	n.s.
Planning	0.32	n.s.
Interpreting	0.54	<0.01
Hypothesizing	0.44	<0.01
Raising questions	0.40	<0.01

In general, there was a trend for the size of the correlation, and hence the extent to which the task demands overlapped, to increase with the cognitive demand of the task. A possible explanation is that for the more complex intellectual tasks such as hypothesizing or raising questions, pupils require a more general 'science reasoning ability' rather than skill in the specific domain. This general science factor is not affected by the mode of presentation (whether the question is given in a written or practical form). A further possible explanation, and one which is very germane to the planning of a national assessment exercise, is that for some domains there may exist what is termed an 'ability mode interaction'. This means that very able pupils might score highly on the written test but poorly on the practical tasks where a low level of science reasoning is required, while the reverse would be true for less able children. This effect would justify Drummond's (1993) plea for alternatives to written examinations for pupils such as Jason.

This possibility of an interaction effect can be explored by examining the correlations between the scores of a particular science domain and the combined scores on the remaining domains (i.e., a person's total score less the person's particular domain score). The higher the correlation the greater the likelihood that an individual with a high score on a particular science process skill also achieves a relatively high score on the combined totals of all the other skills. Such a result would argue for the existence of a common science ability factor which extends across the range of domains rather than indicating that science attainment consists of a series of clearly identifiable traits such as the APU and the SATs procedures suggest. High correlations in both Table 3.1 and Table 3.2 in a domain would indicate the probability of this general factor.

Table 3.2 Intercorrelations between domain scores and the combined total score for written and practical tasks

Domain	Written Task	Practical Task
Observation		0.45
Measuring	0.80	0.34
Recording	0.81	
Planning	0.53	0.80
Interpreting	0.87	0.72
Hypothesizing	0.75	0.62
Raising questions	0.46	0.63

Table 3.2 shows the Pearson r Correlation Coefficients for both the written and the practical exercise. With the relatively small sample size, all the values of the correlations are statistically significant (p less than 0.01, one tailed test). More importantly, the trend is for the size of the correlations in the practical tasks to increase as the cognitive demand becomes greater. The trend for the written exercises is less discernible, partly because opportunities for critical reflection were limited on the written exercise and because the observation scores did not vary among the samples sufficiently to discriminate between high-scoring and low-scoring pupils. The high correlation for the measurement on the written test is explained, in part, because pupils had to carry out this activity as a preliminary to completing the question requiring the interpretation of data. In the practical task, no such guidance was given and pupils had to decide for themselves whether to take a precise measurement in order to carry out the remaining parts of the task.

'Raising questions' on the written test was open-ended where the pupils were expected to generate ideas spontaneously. In the practical task they were prompted by the teacher. While, therefore, because of the differences in the forms of testing the evidence is not totally conclusive, there is a discernible trend in support of the view that tasks requiring higher levels of cognition tend to have a common factor irrespective of the mode in which they are presented. The data do fit the model of the intellect proposed by Gardiner (1983) in which human intelligence is explained in terms which embrace all human activity rather than accounting merely for a narrow specific aptitude. Certain situations require the application of a 'practical intelligence', whereby individuals solve complex intellectual problems in the context of their daily lives while experiencing great difficulty when asked to solve the equivalent problem in a written, decontexualized form. In arithmetic, for example, there are many examples where some individuals can carry out computation mentally in a working context, such as when shopping, yet cannot perform the same sums on paper (Hunter *et al.*, 1993, p.18).

The data in this study were limited by the size of the sample on which the research team was able to carry out sufficient observations. Nevertheless, the results do raise questions about predictive validity, in that, despite annual improvements in the written test scores, observation of lessons showed little change in the use of the process skills during the same period (Cavendish *et al.*, 1990). Similar data collected on a national scale by SEAC could provide more reliable information on these matters; no details of any such analysis have been publicly available. Indeed, Professor Black, on whose recommendations much of the SATs programme was developed, has publicly complained that under the chairmanship of Lord Griffiths, a former Downing Street adviser, there has been a refusal to make any effort to see how the tests were working. Replying to this criticism, Baroness Blatch, at the time acting Secretary of State for Education, explained that, 'It is sad that Professor Black is so badly out of touch' (*The Guardian,* 26 August 1992).

This kind of analysis is important because, if it confirmed the STAR results, it suggests a way out of the present difficulties and provides an alternative to the 'slimming down' proposals in the Dearing Report. For more complex intellectual tasks it appears to make little difference to the result whether the exercise is in a practical or a written mode. In Jason's case, as cited by Drummond (1993), only in those domains having sizeable ability-mode interactions would it be necessary to obtain scores on a practical task. In the case of science this would apply to skills such as observing, recording and measuring, but not to hypothesizing. For other domains, detailed observation of practical tasks would only be carried out in those cases where discrepancies arose between the written test results and the teacher's regular assessments. In a class of 30 pupils this might involve up to six children. This procedure would seem preferable to the highly costly alternative of bringing in external assessors or paying for cover (DfE, 1994).

A weakness of the original TGAT proposals was that they were influenced by similar reasoning to that put forward by Drummond (1933) in her defence of Jason, namely that the test measures used should not advantage some pupils at the expense of others. But it is impracticable to base a national system of assessment on the needs of a minority of pupils like Jason, nor is it necessary. One could go further and say that it is wrong to do so because, by spending the time operating such an elaborate assessment system, teachers are unable to give sufficient attention to the Jasons in their classes. However, the above procedure would only be applicable to the formative assessments which were carried out as part of the school's own programme of accountability, The measurement of national standards presents different problems.

Testing National Standards

In the earlier part of this chapter it was argued that currently there exists no straightforward, practical, analytic method which enables the domain-referenced tests to be used to make summative judgements about the performance of one school relative to another. Standardized tests can be shown to have satisfactory reliability, an essential ingredient of summative assessment (Messick, 1994) but it is often argued that these tests are not 'authentic', i.e., the test requirements do not match the way the content has been taught. Clearly, the situation is easiest in mathematics where there is a degree of curriculum validity between the tasks on the tests and the tasks which are contained in the numerous workbooks which pupils complete as part of the primary mathematics curriculum. The problem then, as Stenberg (1990, p.212) observes, is that both 'test problems' and 'school problems' lack authenticity since they are decontextualized with respect to everyday life problems. In English there are severe problems when assessing for higher level skills involving synthesis and analysis and in devising a satisfactory cost-effective procedure to test oracy.

Science scores are not generalizable across different topics. In the latter case, therefore, the best that can be hoped for is a return to the procedures adopted by the STOS project (Eggleston *et al.*, 1976) where science tests were set within four broad domains: knowledge, problem-solving, experimental design, and hypothesizing and inferring from data. In all cases, apart from the 'knowledge of facts and principles' test, the questions were based on a single theme and the knowledge required was included in the stem of the question. For example, one set of questions on problem-solving dealt with mirrors, and in the stem of the question information about the laws of reflection and refraction were given. There are difficulties in this approach because it places a high premium on the candidate's ability to comprehend the information, but in a simplified form it could be used to test 11-year-old pupils. For this reason, Messick (1994, p.15) suggests a mix of structured items and extended open-ended tasks.

An alternative approach is used as part of the science surveys in the United States carried out by the American College Testing (ACT) Programme (ACT, 1992). Prior to running the bi-annual testing programme, ACT surveys schools in a large number of states and collects curriculum material, including the textbooks used. These are then analysed to ensure that the most common elements within the different curriculum programmes are used for the test items. Another similar system which is used for comparative purposes is the long-established International Project for the Evaluation of Educational Achievement (IEA) study. These evaluations began in the 1960s and have been a regular feature of comparative education in most developed countries. There are problems of interpretation, to do with the sampling procedures, because in some countries where education is highly selective, the pupils taking the tests over-represent the more able within the population in comparison to, say, the United States, where the ability mix is more evenly distributed. Provided that details of the sample are available, there are sets of procedures whereby, unlike the current government league tables, comparisons can be made in ways which take into account these initial inequalities (Goldstein, 1986).

Since the main purpose of the assessment would be to compare schools, and not individual pupils, it would not be necessary for every pupil in the class to take the same test. A system known as 'light' sampling could be used, whereby a series of test papers, containing a selection of the test items, was arranged randomly and distributed in a prearranged order to the class. For example, from a 60-item test, each pupil might be required to answer 10 questions, thus reducing the time and effort required and minimizing the importance of the procedure. The development of such tests and the evaluation of the data could properly be in the hands of an independent body such as the National Foundation for Educational Research which has had long experience in test development of this kind.

Defining National Standards

Once the results have been collected and analysed, a decision must be reached about the standards achieved. Standards are not the same as performance. Schools' scores may increase over time but some judgement must be exercised as to whether the increases are of sufficient magnitude to indicate a national improvement. It was argued earlier in this chapter that the use of the SAT procedure to define national standards is unsatisfactory, in that the argument from which the standard is derived is essentially a circular one. The tests also appear to lack either predictive or construct validity. When determining standards, this type of validity is hard to determine unless it can be based on international comparisons. For example, in the IEA studies a country's test ranking could be used as a predictor of various economic indicators.

Within a single country, however, there is probably little to be done other than by trying to reach an agreed national consensus prior to the testing. One attempt to accomplish this is now the subject of an evaluation in the Netherlands. As described in the previous chapter, the Dutch government instituted a thorough review of their National Curriculum which became law in 1985. In key subjects – mathematics, language, science, geography and history – panels of experts and panels consisting of a cross-section of the wider population (employees, parents, etc.) were separately asked their opinion about the age when pupils should be able to perform a list of tasks and procedures (Van Den Brink and Van Bruggen, 1990).

In many cases there was consensus between the expert and non-expert panels, while in others there were disagreements. For example, the expert panel was satisfied with the levels of mathematics expected of 11-year-olds based on the fact that the Dutch pupils appeared in the first half dozen countries of the most recent IEA mathematics study. Employees and parents, however, wanted higher levels of performance. In geography, the reverse happened, where employers and parents were content with knowledge that was mainly local or national, whereas experts thought it important that Dutch pupils should acquire an international perspective. In cases of disagreement, matters will be referred to the government for a final decision, After three years these standards will be reviewed by similar panels and the levels reset in the light of school performance and national needs. The Netherlands also participates in the IEA evaluation surveys.

If similar procedures were to be adopted here in the UK, it would require national testing at age 7 to be abandoned other than for formative purposes and for reporting to parents. The unreliability of written procedure at this age would require any assessment to be based upon a large amount of systematic observation, necessitating considerable cost and effort. Probably all that can reasonably be done at the national level is to produce an agreed set of 'benchmark' measures, with schools reporting the age at which each of its pupils achieves these requirements. A similar conclusion is reached by Torrance (1991). A number of continental European countries, including The Netherlands, have also adopted this strategy.

Chapter 4
Three Unwise Men?

One of the aims of those who conceived the idea of a National Curriculum was to raise standards by ending the influence on primary practice of what was referred to as 'Plowdenism'. According to Duncan Graham's account of these developments, things began to go wrong, as far as he was concerned, when Kenneth Clarke replaced John McGregor as Secretary of State for Education. According to Graham, the junior ministers, particularly Tim Eggar, 'saw every initiative as dangerous'. In spite of the evidence to the contrary, NCC was seen as being in the hands of the professionals, the educationalists and the teachers. These two ministers moved in every direction to curtail the activities of the Council, particularly in the publication of documents. On one occasion Eggar asked,

> Why over the last two years had the Council not taken steps to simplify the curriculum, why had it allowed it to become even more complicated and why had the Council *not sorted out the way the teachers taught?* (*The Guardian*, 13 October 1992, emphasis added)

This key phrase, 'sorting out the way teachers taught' strongly supports the argument in Chapter 2 that education ministers saw the National Curriculum as providing not a *framework* but a *straitjacket* whereby teachers would be forced to revert to more traditional ways of teaching. Shortly after Kenneth Clarke's arrival at Elizabeth House, ministers were said to be interested in issues of teaching and were open to various views. The catalyst for Eggar's outburst to Duncan Graham was the publication in May 1991 of *Primary Education in Leeds,* the Twelfth and Final Report from the Primary Needs Independent Evaluation Project directed by Robin Alexander (Alexander, 1991). This summary document became something of a 'cause célèbre', at times taking on the dimension of a report from a Royal Commission. Ministers focused on the general finding that for an estimated expenditure of £13.75 million, over a five-year period from 1985 to 1990, the evaluators were unable to discover significant shifts towards more effective patterns of classroom organization or improvement in outcomes such as reading. A major reason for this failure, according to Alexander was because

> the programme and indeed wider aspects of the authority's approach to primary education was centralised to an excessive degree and that this generated reactions from Heads and teachers which were both powerful and counter-productive. Most of the teachers concerns centred on what they saw as in imposition from above of a particular version of 'good primary practice' and the relationship of teachers' allegiance of this to career prospects. (Alexander, 1991, p.143)

Elsewhere, Alexander argues that this notion 'of good primary practice' placed teachers under pressure to adopt strategies whose efficacy

> ... we have shown to be debatable. The most notable examples were grouping, the practice of having a multiple curriculum focus in teaching sessions with different groups working in different curriculum areas and kinds of teacher-pupil interaction associated with a commitment to discovery learning. (Alexander, 1991, p.137)

Perhaps the most worrying result, for a government wedded to improving standards, was the finding that,

> Reading scores at 7+ and 9+ from 1983–91 showed no evidence that the injection of extra staff and money into Leeds Primary Schools, especially those in the Inner City, had a positive impact on children's reading ability, at least as measured by the authority's test. On the contrary, scores showed a decline towards the end of the evaluation period, especially in the Inner City schools where PNP [Primary Needs Programme] resources were concentrated. (Alexander, 1991, p.l36)

The government's response was to invite Professor Alexander, along with Christopher Woodhead, the then chief executive of the National Curriculum Council and Jim Rose, Senior Primary Inspector, to produce a report summarizing existing research on teaching in primary schools. Speed was to be of the essence: the authors were given six weeks in which to carry out their review. Once the report was in government hands, it was then rushed out in typescript for a press conference two weeks before it was available for distribution to schools (Simon, 1993). Simon describes this press conference where the education correspondents were given 15 minutes to read the report which consisted of at least 20,000 words. According to one of the reporters who was present, they were told by Kenneth Clarke, 'Don't bother to read the document. You will find the bullet points made in my press release'. All this, argues Simon, was 'symptomatic of the level and character of current Ministerial behaviour' (Simon, 1993, p.13).

The report was the culmination of what Simon describes as 'a coordinated onslaught' on primary practice by politicians (or rather ministers) backed up, of course, by the tabloid press. Simon quotes Michael Fallon announcing that,

the days of group project work were numbered; that teachers should forget the 'fiction of child centred learning' and 'the pursuit of happiness' and concentrate instead on individual subject learning and whole class teaching.

This was followed by a further critique in *The Times,* where Kenneth Clarke claimed, 'There is a great deal of play centred teaching' and, at is weakest, 'There is a lot of sticking together egg boxes and playing in sand' (Simon, 1993, p.13).

The criticism was not only restricted to the government side. The then opposition education spokesman, Jack Straw, came out in support of the call by the general secretary of the National Association of Headteachers, David Hart, for the reintroduction of streaming at the top end of junior school. Straw argued that 'gifted children should be placed in "fast streams"', and that a future Labour Government 'would ensure that pupils, particularly in primary schools were no longer taught in mixed ability groups or by age' (Simon, 1993, p.13). It was at this point that Kenneth Clarke released his 6,000-word statement on primary practice quoting various researchers and making his own views very clear, before announcing the appointment of what came to be known as the 'Three Wise Men'. Yet even before the report was published, there were rumours in the press that two of the three authors were already in fundamental disagreement over the interpretation of the evidence and the purpose of the exercise. This led *The Education Guardian* to publish statements on the report by both Professor Alexander and Christopher Woodhead and to feature a comment in an editorial under the heading, 'One Unwise Man', saying of Alexander, 'To write one report and deny its consequences is unfortunate. To write two and deny them both is unforgivable' (*The Guardian*, 12 February 1992, p.18). Alexander's alleged fault was to have signed the report but then attempted, subsequently, to play down the significance of its findings under pressure from 'his peers in the educational world'. This charge was vigorously denied in a letter to the editor (*The Guardian*, 14 February 1992, p.20).

A characteristic of the report's reception in the media was the concentration on Woodhead's allegation that there were certain 'mediocre schools' which, while not espousing a child-centred philosophy, nevertheless 'fail their children'. Apart from the editor of *The Independent*, no one seemed prepared to give Professor Alexander's case a sympathetic hearing. *The Guardian,* which during similar debates in the 1980s had defended primary teaching, strongly endorsed the report, and continued to attack Professor Alexander, arguing that he,

> should read yesterday's accompanying feature by Chris Woodhead, another
> of the holy trio, who was much more frank about the weaknesses as well as
> the strengths, of present primary teaching force. [The writer then concluded]
> Of course, it is tough to swim against the tide, but Robin Alexander has the
> perfect surfboard: the detailed facts that he uncovered in his five year study
> in Leeds. Such facts are sacred as a guide to action. (*The Guardian*, 12
> February 1992, p.18)

Over the next week the press, and *The Guardian* in particular, continued
to mount this campaign. Woodhead's views went uncriticized. He began
his *Guardian* comments by stating that the 'reality of the problem
facing primary education' was brought home to him by an overheard
telephone conversation of an American 7-year-old, who was spending a
term in a London primary school. She told her father that 'she was
enjoying herself but felt a little bored. The teachers didn't teach her
anything' (*The Guardian*, 11 February, p.21). In the same article
Woodhead also went on to talk about 'longstanding friends' who,
although committed to state education, 'have expressed their guilt at
how close they are to moving their children into private schooling'. His
remarks, particularly the phrase, 'reality of the situation', coupled with
the emotive claim that some teachers 'fail their children', tended to
create an impression that the situation was critical and set the tone of
the subsequent debate in the press. Alexander's plea, that policy makers,
as well as those in schools, should also look for the reasons why
primary practice was not as effective as it might be, was generally
ignored. Woodhead, for example, had little to say about the impact of
the National Curriculum other than to claim that it was the key to
improved practice. He went on to argue that the acquisition by teachers
of greater subject knowledge was another important means of
promoting school improvement, along with the need to keep the
National Curriculum under constant review. The article concluded with
a strong plea for a shift to school-based teacher training, despite the
criticisms of existing practice in the report! Woodhead's views were
interpreted as reflecting the government's intended message (*The
Guardian*, 11 February 1992, p.3). It is not hard to see why, given this
interpretation of events, concerns were later expressed that, 'with a low
profile chief executive', the transformed NCC might become the
'Secretary of State's poodle' (Watkins, 1993, p.16).

In the same week, Alexander was again attacked in the newspaper,
this time by Melonie Phillips (*The Guardian*, 14 February 1992, p.20).
Phillips pointed to a particular statement from the 'Three Wise Men's'

report which claimed that 'much teaching in primary schools has suffered from highly questionable dogmas which have generated progressively complex classroom practice and devalued the role of subjects in the curriculum'. Asked to expand on this statement at the press conference, Professor Alexander had replied that these 'questionable dogmas were less widespread than may be thought'. 'Why then', asked Philips, 'did he write "much teaching has suffered from them" if the dogmas had been exaggerated? Why is Professor Alexander so terrified of his own conclusions since no politician, clearly, is putting the frightners on?'

Phillips' own explanation, for what she regarded as Alexander's curious behaviour, then followed:

It must surely be that his final report swims against current orthodoxy and has upset his peers in the education world. It takes courage to put your head above the parapet and keep it there. He is, therefore, saying to the teachers, 'Don't trust what you think I wrote: believe instead what I am telling you I wrote.' But he did write it. Don't trust this revisionist who writes for newspapers using the name of the excellent Professor Robin Alexander. (*The Guardian*, 14 February 1992, p.20).

It may be, as Simon (1993, p.13) concluded, 'that the whole exercise should be seen in terms of power struggles within the governing [Conservative] party'. Given that the post of Secretary of State for Education has often been regarded as a stepping stone to higher things (Kenneth Baker went to the Home Office, Kenneth Clarke eventually to the Treasury), each education minister, according to Simon, 'must make his mark and above all enhance his reputation amongst the more important of the warring elements'. Accordingly,

Crises are therefore conjured up out of nowhere providing opportunities for Napoleonic gestures in response. So the Minister gains prestige (in this case among the right wing of his party) strengthening his claims for further advancement should the opportunity arise. (Simon, 1993, p.13)

Simon may well be right, since Mr Clarke's successor, John Patten, almost immediately he took office, shifted attention to Key Stage 3 and to 'opting out' of LEA control. But the attacks on primary practice can also be seen as part of a well-organized campaign which seeks a return to what were perceived to be the halcyon days before the Plowden Report, of which the latest move in the campaign has been Dearing's offer of '20 per cent time' for non-core subjects. The lack of any serious questioning of its recommendations, or the premises on which these were based, means that as the 'Three Wise Men's' document becomes part of contemporary primary history, it will be regarded as an essentially valid analysis. There is a danger, therefore, that next time primary pedagogy becomes a national issue, the need for whole-class teaching with greater subject specialization will have been uncritically accepted and those who attempt to argue for a different approach will be regarded as being 'out of touch' with reality. It was perhaps this fear which lead Professor Alexander to react to the publication of his report in ways that made it appear that he was 'backtracking' on its conclusions and drew down the wrath of the media upon his head.

Before attempting a detailed critical analysis of the report, however, it is necessary to look closely at the catalyst which sparked the debate: Alexander's own study of primary education in Leeds. The publication of its final evaluation report brought the 'Three Wise Men' into existence and provided a focus for the government's attack on LEAs and on university departments of education. Again, surprisingly for such a detailed study, there has been very little analysis of the report's findings or its methodology. Perhaps, because some of the findings on classroom practice replicated earlier research, Alexander's interpretation has remained unchallenged. Yet, it is not difficult to argue that, in some important instances, the methods of analysis used by Alexander and his team were relatively unsophisticated and that, therefore, the evaluation's conclusions should be regarded more tentatively than has so far been the case.

Primary Education in Leeds

In 1985 Leeds City Council established the Primary Needs Programme (PNP). PNP sought to meet the needs of every child in the city's primary schools, improve practice and enhance the relationships between the school, home and the community. The inauguration of the project coincided with the appointment of a new senior primary adviser, John Rawlinson, who had previously held a similar post in Salford where the mainly inner-city primary schools had attracted a good deal of favourable comment. In the first year of the programme, Leicester University School of Education was commissioned to provide courses for headteachers and for the primary needs coordinators who were appointed in every school. The coordinators' course was directed by Dr Pat Ashton whose earlier work for the Open University came to be known as the 'Curriculum in Action' Project. This led her to establish, on her move to Leicester, The Centre for Evaluation and Development in Teacher Education, based upon similar principles. For headteachers, the course was planned and coordinated by a number of headteachers who had previously been involved in various ORACLE projects. Both courses achieved only limited success with the better evaluations coming from the coordinators rather than from the headteachers. Indeed, for much of the year, Ashton and her colleagues found themselves taking on the role of counsellors rather than curriculum developers because of the difficulties experienced by these coordinators when they attempted to carry out their duties. In some cases, coordinators did not managed to gain entry into any classrooms throughout the entire first year of the programme!

Part of the reason for these difficulties was because the coordinators were named after the project and called 'primary needs coordinators'. This suggested that they were specifically concerned with children identified as having 'special learning needs'. Since most of the schools involved had arrangements where children with learning difficulties were withdrawn from normal classes, the coordinators were perceived as an additional 'pair of hands' to help with this task. Their advisory role was, therefore, perceived to be concerned with this aspect of the school's work and this only. During the first year several strategies were devised, with the help of Pat Ashton, to win over the confidence of teachers within the school, some of whom resented the fact that the coordinators were earning larger salaries. Some of these long-serving staff openly challenged the competence of their new colleagues who, in some cases, had not previously taught 'inner-city' children. Most primary needs coordinators spent much of the first year attempting to establish their credibility as effective practitioners by volunteering to act as supply teachers whenever someone was absent.

Not surprisingly, there was even more resentment among the group of headteachers who felt that their schools had been specially targeted as needing improvement. They viewed the newly-assigned coordinators as supernumeraries who had been put into their schools to do a job that they and their deputy headteachers had failed to do. Efforts to create discussion groups to share experiences and to look at some of the issues involved in school leadership and curriculum change were resisted on the grounds that this was not what the project was about. The headteachers, who were helping to tutor this part of the course, operated in their own schools through a system of 'power sharing' which is usually now described as 'collegial' (Fullan and Hargreaves, 1992; Nias et al., 1989). These tutors were, in the main, very critical of the professionalism exhibited by their Leeds counterparts. Teacher coordinators from these tutors' schools, who took part in one session, remarked that they would be very reluctant to work for all but a few of these Leeds headteachers!

The purpose in providing this description of the first year's events is to put the evaluation subsequently carried out by Robin Alexander and his colleagues in context. This is all the more necessary given the importance attached by government ministers to Alexander's forthright criticisms of the LEA's methods (and therefore, by implication, John Rawlinson and his advisory colleagues). The PRINDEP final evaluation report goes some way, in its opening paragraphs, to acknowledge the difficulties initially facing the LEA advisers. The report referred to the low levels of 'per capita educational spending' and 'high teacher pupil ratios'. It noted that the authority operated a 'ring fence' policy on new primary teacher appointments and that the advisory and support services were in comparison with many other LEAs, 'very thin'. The system was perceived to have been 'stagnant and old fashioned' (Alexander, 1991, p.7). In short, it would appear that in some respects Leeds schools and its teaching staff were atypical. This much can at least be claimed when Alexander's rather 'coded' messages are combined with the earlier Leicester experience.

It was, therefore, unfortunate that the evaluation team was not in place until towards the end of this first year, since this initial phase of the programme went unreported. There was nothing to balance the various critical comments throughout the evaluation as to 'the persistence of ambiguities in policy and confusion in teachers' understanding of PNP' which it was claimed 'continued to generate tension for the entire four year period of the Primary Needs Independent Evaluation Project (PRINDEP) evaluation' (Alexander, 1991, p.8). Neither were detailed case studies possible, showing what schools were like at the beginning of the project in comparison to the final phase and, therefore, no measure of how far the authority had succeeded in moving schools, given that their initial 'low base' appeared to be very low indeed. The initial context may also have helped explain some of the decisions taken by the senior primary adviser and his team, decisions which were subsequently criticized in the evaluation report 'as imposing too rigid a view of "good practice"'.

The LEA was also criticized for the 'persistence of ambiguities in policy'. This serious indictment needs to be set against Alexander's writing over the same period where uncertainties of a similar kind, as to the best ways to improve practice, can also be detected. At the beginning of the evaluation, when comparing the world of informal primary education to either a garden or a jungle, Alexander (1988) noted the 'randomness of personal experience' (p.159) and the way in which this required those planning primary education to respond flexibly. The form primary education takes can therefore change markedly 'from one curriculum area to another' (p.173). In the same article, Alexander also criticized the ideological pressures which developed from the ORACLE research that children should not be in groups unless they were working cooperatively (p.178). He also attacked the notion that 'higher order cognitive interactions' should be regarded 'as a prerequisite for purposeful learning' (p.180).

Here, then, at least by implication, Alexander seems to be arguing for acceptance and understanding of existing practice whereby teachers, because they use different organizational arrangements for different 'curriculum areas', frequently need to engage their pupils in less demanding activities consisting, in the main, of factual and routine instruction. A year later, however, when the results of the first phase of the project were published, references to the value of group work were now less hostile and instead (Alexander *et al.,* 1989, pp.256–7), discussion was concerned with the dilemmas facing teachers when attempting to use a group strategy effectively. Concern, however, was still expressed over the misinterpretations which can arise over ambiguities in the messages delivered to teachers from those providing the courses. By the end of the evaluation, however, 'higher order cognitive interactions' were once more in favour. Alexander was now arguing,

> for more questions of a kind which encourage children to reason and speculate; for more opportunities for children themselves to ask their own questions and have these addressed; for oral feedback to children which without being negative is more exact and informative than mere praise; and for much more use of *structured pupil-pupil interaction*, both as a learning tool and as a means of helping teachers to function in a more considered manner and therefore more effectively. (Alexander 1991, p.138, emphasis added)

This view changes to a more prescriptive one within the 'Three Wise Men's' report. These recommendations now stress the value of subject specialist class-based teaching and thus place greater emphasis on *teacher-pupil* rather than *pupil-pupil* interactions (Alexander *et al.,* 1992).

The above paragraphs are not meant to be over-critical nor indeed hostile of Alexander's views. Reading the many publications written during the period of the evaluation, particularly the working documents, provides a fascinating glimpse of someone struggling to come to terms with a whole range of questions concerning the ways primary teachers think about practice and the relation of these thoughts to actions. Alexander is particularly interesting when teasing out the various dilemmas facing primary teachers: the endless compromises needed to construct a workable curriculum which allows them to function in a reasonable manner but, at the same time, necessitates pupils engaging in 'time-filling' activities. But what remains puzzling to the reader is why Alexander does not also attempt to map out, in a similar manner, the personal 'journey of discovery' of the advisers whose work he so strongly criticizes. The advisory team must have faced equally difficult professional and also political dilemmas at a time when the National Curriculum was being superimposed on to the INSET activities of the Primary Needs Programme, activities which produced 'confusing messages'. The evaluation, therefore, appears to operate at different times within different methodologies. When writing about teachers and schools, Alexander is the researcher, attempting to place his findings carefully within a context. When dealing with the LEA, however, his stance seems closer to that of HMI who, on school inspections, merely 'report what we see'.

To take a specific example, consider the criticism levelled at the authority for imposing too rigid a view of good practice. Elsewhere, Alexander (1988) has written that one of the major difficulties facing those wishing to promote change in primary schools is the hybrid nature of contemporary classroom practice which results in the merger of both competing and conflicting ideologies. The result of this 'hybridization', as explained in Chapter 1, is that the messages being received by schools are inevitably, to a degree, unclear. When these messages are then subjected to the individual teacher's personal interpretation, the result is likely to be a *laissez-faire* approach to primary practice, commonly identified in earlier studies (Richards, 1982). One critical area involves the form and content of INSET offered to primary teachers. Typically, little guidance is given to the visiting tutor providing the programme; certainly none will concern pedagogic issues. Thus a tutor, charged with introducing a new activity in mathematics, will set these ideas within his or her own preconceived views about the best way to organize the classroom and the appropriate teaching strategies that should be employed. Another teacher attending an arts course, from the same school where a colleague took part in the mathematics INSET, may be advised to use a different teaching approach. When these different experiences are shared with colleagues back at the school, it is not altogether surprising that a general view emerges that methods of organization and teaching strategies are a matter of personal preference. Headteachers will, accordingly, allow each member of staff to exercise their own independent judgement in matters of teaching style.

Faced with a need to change this situation, because the personal preferences of Leeds teachers appeared to provide a general level of practice that, in Alexander's words, provided 'a very low base', it is not surprising that the local authority decided to concentrate on what they saw as one or two key areas. In this way everyone involved in the Primary Needs Programme would be 'singing the same tune'. The choice of areas: flexibility of classroom organization, adapting the classroom to the needs of the curriculum and increased levels of pupil-pupil interaction, would seem to have been an informed one. For over a decade, classroom researchers had pointed to the excessive amounts of 'busy work' which accompanied the use of individual instruction in primary classrooms. Alexander, himself, had earlier succinctly described such activity as 'adequate if undemanding' (Alexander, 1984). Add to this the fact that whole-class teaching approaches would have had to operate within a complex system of organization where pupils were in mixed-age, mixed-ability groups, and the emphasis given to collaborative forms of group work becomes easy to understand. It may be, as Alexander claims, that the way in which this message was imparted left something to be desired. But in his analysis of the teachers and their schools, Alexander criticizes other classroom researchers for taking 'little account of the teacher's intention in offering its characteri-sation in critiques of their practices' (Alexander, 1988, p.178). It is clearly legitimate to enquire why similar strictures should not apply in the present case, where no detailed indication is given in the evaluation report of the thinking of the planning team who managed the Primary Needs Programme.

Instead, the Final Report (Alexander, 1991) made repeated, strongly worded, criticisms of the LEA's part in the programme. It is accused of being 'too interventionist' (Alexander, 1992, p.119), of creating a climate where it was the 'main definer and arbiter of good practice' and where this 'firm stance on good practice taken by the authority's advisory staff was inseparable from the part they played both in the formal processes of promotion and appointment' (p.120), and where the approach to the curriculum was 'strong on rhetoric about the whole but weak on details about specifics', and where 'such specifics appeared to receive attention in a fairly random way' (p.123). This charge, that the LEA, presumably through its advisory team, pursued a policy of imposing good practice, based on ideology rather than pragmatism, was particularly damning in view of the use made of it subsequently by government ministers. An attempt, somewhere in the Report, to balance this criticism with an explanation of the thinking on which the advisers' actions were based, might well have been prudent as well as method-ologically correct.

In concluding this part of the critique, it should be said that there is little evidence from elsewhere that other forms of INSET, particularly that described as 'school-focused' or 'school-based' which Alexander (1992, p.133) recommends, have proven more successful in changing practice. Programmes based upon the model developed by Ashton *et al.* (1989) for IT-INSET were unable to demonstrate any improvement in performance, other than the students' and teachers' perceptions of greater satisfaction and confidence. Elsewhere, school-focused programmes based upon notions of 'critical reflection' and 'action research' have also appeared to have enjoyed only limited success (Galton and Williamson, 1992, pp.181–4). Given that, at the time, there was no consensus operating either in the UK, the USA or continental Europe about the best way to encourage curriculum reform (Galton and Blyth, 1989), the confusion and uncertainty generated by the Leeds programme should not have come as a total surprise to the evaluation team, particularly since these attempted improvements in classroom pedagogy had to be subsumed within the statutory requirement to support the introduction of the National Curriculum. Overall, therefore, the evaluation is less than generous in attempting to understand the LEA perspective.

There are two other areas of the PNP evaluation which, it can be argued, give rise to concern. The first concern has to do with the 'tone' generated by the language used to represent some teachers' views as well a doubts about the validity of certain interpretations. The second concern, the more substantial one, has to do with the limitations of the methods used to analyse the empirical data on reading progress.

Within certain sections of the report the language used may, with hindsight, be seen to have too readily fed the prejudices of both the 'New Right' and government ministers and helped set the tone of the subsequent debate in the media to which Alexander objected. It is now generally accepted that an evaluator can never adopt a 'neutral' or 'apolitical' stance, but he or she does have an obligation of anticipating the 'clients" reactions and of choosing words carefully so that sections from the report cannot easily be used out of context. In this way the evaluator attempts to be fair to all sides. How, then, is a reader, particular one unsympathetic to modern primary methods, likely to react to the following discussion of the way some teachers use rhetoric to describe primary practice?

> As a general rule, the more purist and dogmatic the value orientation of the Head, the bigger the discrepancy with observed practice. In these cases, a school philosophy acquired a life of its own: paraded for Governors, advisers, parents and visitors, reflected superficially in those aspects of practice like display and decor that such outsiders tended immediately to note, but seldom follow through. (Alexander, 1991, p.103)

The passage is very effectively crafted and headteachers of such disposition present an easy target. The net effect of the paragraph could be for critics of contemporary primary schooling to perceive such school leaders as gullible, unintelligent teachers absorbing the LEA's ideology uncritically. Such readers might perhaps conclude that the greater the dose of ideology offered, the greater the gullibility (and perhaps, therefore, stupidity) of the headteacher and the less effective the school. In Chapter 1, however, it was argued that practice and ideology are not so closely linked and that strategic pedagogic decisions often derive largely from pragmatism. If this is the case, then the above interpretation may not be the whole story.

In many cases ideology is often used as justification of one's professionally 'espoused theory' (Eraut, 1994, p.29). To regard teaching as a profession requires that its practitioners should know something about the way their actions are underpinned by theoretical constructs. To accept less would be to reduce teaching to a technical procedure. Lacking a clear language to describe both pedagogy and learning (Simon, 1981b), teachers may have recourse to rhetoric, and since advisers by and large are ex-teachers, they will also operate within this same framework of professional discourse. To observe, as Alexander does, that there is a huge gap between this professional discourse and the classroom, and that teachers who engage in the most rhetoric are closer to 'normative' practice, is, in effect, to concede the proposition that practice is pragmatically driven. Given Alexander's strong criticisms of the way in which the media used his reports, particularly on the matter of ideologically-driven practice, the issues developed here did perhaps require a more penetrating analysis in the evaluation report, if only in the interests of balance. The style of presentation also, in retrospect, might have been reviewed.

A more important concern, however, has to do with procedures used to analyse the reading data. The raw data consisted of the reading scores collected by the authority for 7-plus and 9-plus children. The evaluation team collected and computer analysed all the available test scores from 1983 to 1989 in order to gain a view of the trends in each Primary Needs Programme phase across all 230 of the authority's primary schools (Alexander, 1991, p.51). In the final report the analysis is illustrated by two tables in which the overall means and standard deviations coinciding with each phase of the Primary Needs Programme were presented. The report noted that the position in Leeds was comparable to that elsewhere in the country, with an apparent decline in reading standards over the last few years. Unlike other parts of the country, as reported by the NFER (Cato and Whetton, 1990), the decline in Leeds appeared greatest in the inner-city schools where the PNP programme was supposed to have the greatest impact. Alexander concluded that,

> It is clear that the massive injection of staff and material resources under the Primary Needs Programme had no perceivable impact on reading standards overall although the school by school figures do show considerable improvements in some cases in deterioration. This means that if reading standards are taken as a measure of PNP's success then the programme in this respect, at least, must be counted a failure. However, it is also possible that without PNP any downward trend would have been even more marked. (Alexander, 1991, p.54, para 399.10)

Although this statement is subject to a degree of qualification, it stands as a damning indictment of the PNP project, not withstanding the 20-odd positive findings. Given the importance attached to standards of reading by the media and the government, it is puzzling that only the tables presented in the final report should consist of crude comparisons of year-by-year mean reading scores. The evaluation was unusual in not seeking to relate these reading outcomes to the classroom process information collected throughout the study. Looking back to previous studies which sought to identify links between primary practice and pupil performance, it is not difficult to detect an increasing sophistication in the kinds of analysis undertaken. Galton and Simon (1980) used what is known as 'covariance analysis'; the limitations of this approach were discussed by the authors (pp.58–9). In the ORACLE study, covariance analysis, based upon both individual scores and whole class scores, was carried out to show that the trends were the same in both cases. The ORACLE research also set up a series of hypotheses which might explain these observed differences in progress. By determining the degree of variation that each of these predicted explanations accounted for, it was possible to estimate their influence on the test scores. In this way, for example, differences between single-age and mixed-age classes were found to be significant (Galton and Croll, 1980).

More recently, new procedures have been developed, some of which were tried out in the study conducted by Barbara Tizard (Tizard *et al.*, 1988). These procedures allow sample means to be adjusted to compensate for small numbers on which some may be based. Within such 'multi-level models' it is possible not only to look for differences across schools and across classes but also between different kinds of pupils within the schools (e.g., low versus high ability; male and female pupils, etc.).

Without knowing how the LEA data were stored, it is not possible to determine whether different levels of analysis could have been pursued.

Original data were available for a large number of pupils since 'PRINDEP collated and computer analysed all test scores for the six years 1983–89 – some 85,000 in all. No sample was drawn. Every child's score was included' (para 396). With such a database it should have been possible to do an altogether different kind of analysis using the multi-level modelling techniques recently developed. This would have made it possible to identify schools where the greatest progress had been made and then to look at the case study material for reasons why these schools differed from others. For example, were the schools where headteachers offered the highest levels of rhetoric also those in which little progress occurred? Did the strategy adopted by a particular coordinator have an effect? At the next level, that of the class, particular questions about teacher performance could have been considered, rather than accounting for the ineffectiveness of the PNP programme in terms of INSET, ideology or generalized descriptions of classroom practice. At pupil level even more detailed explanations might have been forthcoming. Were certain groups of pupils within a school particularly disadvantaged? How did individual progress relate to such factors as class size, proportion of time pupils spent working on relevant tasks, the proportions of class and group teaching experienced? The latter two variables are particularly important, given the subsequent recommendations of the 'Three Wise Men'. Such analysis would have provided a wealth of detailed information which might have prevented the results being interpreted by the media in the way that Alexander subsequently complained about.

It can be argued, therefore, that the Primary Education in Leeds evaluation team brought some of the resulting problems upon their own heads by not anticipating the likely consequences of their report in those areas which subsequently became the focus of controversy. However, it would be unfair to go so far as Hammersley and Scarth (1993) who imply that Alexander, as one of the co-authors of the 'Three Wise Men's' report, was unwise to involve his own PNP evaluation in an enterprise,

> which smacks of an attitude towards professionalism in education and other fields that seems to have become all too common over the past decade or so in Government circles; it is an attitude which exudes dogmatism. (Hammersley and Scarth, 1993, p.496)

These critics clearly underestimate the dilemma facing Robin Alexander when invited by Kenneth Clarke to take part in the 'Three Wise Men's' review. They are also in the comfortable position, in making their criticisms, of never having done a similar large-scale empirical research with such sensitive national policy implications. But the criticism Hammersley and Scarth make concerning over-interpretation of the evidence to support a particular view, together with a lack of 'judicious awareness' of methodological problems also need to be considered with respect to the PNP evaluation report, since it had a major impact on what was to follow. This applies, particularly, to the criticisms made by Alexander and his team, of the LEA, their treatment of reading performance and the perceived effects of progressivism – what later in the 'Three Wise Men's' report was to be termed 'Plowdenism'. When, as one of this trio, Alexander attempted to advise those seeking to interpret the PNP findings too critically, to exercise a degree of caution of the kind discussed in this chapter, it was alleged that he had opened up 'serious divisions with his co-authors' (*The Guardian*, 11 February 1992, p.2). When at the subsequent press conference he again attempted to present a balanced view, he was attacked and pilloried by the media. By then, as will now be demonstrated, it was too late to prevent his criticisms of primary education in Leeds from being extrapolated to include the whole of primary education.

The Three Wise Men's Report

The stated purpose of the discussion paper, *Curriculum Organisation and Classroom Practice in Primary Schools,* (Alexander *et al.*, 1992) was to 'review available evidence about the delivery of education in primary schools' in order to 'make recommendations about curriculum organisation, teaching methods and classroom practice appropriate for the successful implementation of the National Curriculum, particularly in Key Stage 2'. The main findings of what came to be called by the media the 'Three Wise Men's' report were (i) that it was possible to identify some evidence of downward trends of important aspects of literacy and numeracy (paras 32–5); (ii) that the influence of highly questionable dogmas had led to excessively complex classroom practices and devalued the place of subjects in the curriculum (paras 62–4); (iii) that there was clear evidence to show that much topic work lead to fragmentary and superficial teaching (para 68); and (iv) that the organizational strategy of whole-class, group work and individual teaching needed to be used more selectively and flexibly, the criterion of choice being fitness for purpose. In particular, the three authors argued that in many schools the benefits of whole-class teaching had been insufficiently exploited (paras 86–101).

On the issue of subject expertise needed for primary teaching, the report concluded that the National Curriculum required the introduction of semi-specialist and specialist teachers into primary schools with a strong case for concentrating specialist teaching at the upper end of Key Stage 2 (paras 139–50). On training, the report argued for better articulation of the respective roles of initial teacher training, induction and INSET and that at initial training and induction stages the major purpose should be the acquisition and strengthening of subject expertise, with broad training in a range of classroom organizational strategies and teaching techniques (paras 164–9).

The first part of the report, 'Primary Education in the 1990s' summarizes the evidence and attempts (paras 6–23) to distance the discussion from the previous debates in which primary teaching was largely polarized into either progressive or traditional modes. Although Alexander (*The Guardian*, 14 February 1992, p.20) made it clear that he fully endorsed the report's contents, one of the main fascinations for the reader is to speculate as to which of the trio was responsible for drafting particular sections. In general, it can be surmised that the more scholarly and reflective writing was probably done by Alexander; the more general paragraphs on assessment practice, subject matter and training were the responsibility of the HMI, leaving, perhaps, the more strongly expressed criticisms of existing practice to come from the chief executive of the NCC.

This first section was, therefore, probably drafted by Alexander with little contribution from his co-authors. However, it is likely that drafting Section 3, 'Standards of Achievement in Primary Schools' (paras 24–50), because of its great political sensitivity, was undertaken by Alexander's two colleagues, probably the HMI. The section looks at the evidence for falling standards. Not surprisingly, given the discussion in the previous chapter, the analysis based upon the Assessment and Performance Unit data, standardized tests from LEAs and the National Foundation for Educational Research, and the recent SATs, provided a very mixed set of results from which to reach firm statements about primary pupils' progress over the previous decade. The writer(s) seems unaware of the underlying assumptions governing the APU and SATs measures in basing their analysis (paras 38–43) on the percentages of pupils who achieved different levels of performance. As was suggested in Chapter 3, these levels were predetermined by the pilot study and the argument based upon these percentages is, therefore, a circular one. Once this view is accepted there is little justification for statements of the kind: 'pupils did less well than expected in number operations' (Attainment Target 3) where 44 per cent had not yet reached Level 2 (para 40). On the basis of the evidence, presented in Chapter 3, all that can be validly concluded is that compared to the pilot sample, which may or may not have been a reasonable representation of the population of primary children, the test when given to all 7-year-old pupils, produced lower scores. How far this had to do with sampling error, the unreliability of the measures used, the variation in the way in which the tests were administered or reflected a genuine difference, it is not possible to say.

Nowhere in the report is any direct criticism made of these attainment measures, although their weaknesses are implied in the rather tentative manner in which conclusions are offered. The only telling piece of evidence is the NFER reading test taken by 8-year-olds in 1991 where, compared to 1987, there was the 4.5 standard points decline in the average reading scores (para 37). This period of testing, however, coincided with the introduction of the National Curriculum. Given the findings of Campbell and Neill (1992) and Webb (1993) on the difficulties confronting teachers throughout this period, it is an equally plausible explanation that the apparent 'hiatus' in reading progress was due to the very reforms which were supposed to 'raise standards'! Evidence to support the claim for falling standards, therefore, relies heavily on HMI's conclusion, based on inspections, that wide variations in standards of pupil achievement between schools serving similar catchment areas, had been observed (para 440). Finally, an attempt at some international comparisons is made (paras 47–9) with data from the early 1980s. However, it is admitted that this analysis was highly unreliable given the sampling differences across different countries. In summary, therefore, Hammersley and Scarth (1993) do have a point on the question of falling standards, when arguing that the evidence did not altogether justify the conclusion (para 2) that 'it is possible to identify some evidence of downward trends in important aspects of literacy and numeracy'.

Section 4 deals with the quality of teaching in the primary classroom. It is at this section that Hammersley and Scarth direct their strongest criticisms, claiming that the evidence on which this section was based is problematic. Much of the evidence used by the writer of this section (again, probably Alexander) has been cited in the earlier chapters of this book, particularly the work of Bennett (1976, 1991). Campbell (1985), Campbell and Neill (1992), Galton (1989), Galton and Patrick (1990), Galton and Williamson (1992), Mortimore et al. (1988), Tizard et al. (1988) plus, of course, Alexander's (1991) Leeds study. Taken together, this research has provided a consistent picture of life in primary classrooms spanning nearly two decades. Yet Hammersley and Scarth, in questioning the evidence, mainly focus on the earliest of these researches, Bennett's (1976) work. They return to criticisms by Gray and Satterley (1976) but make no reference to Anthony's (1982) contribution to this debate showing how Bennett's and Gray's results might be reconciled. In any case, Gray's study, part of his PhD, was very small scale and hardly merits the weight given to it by Hammersley and Scarth. They also attempt to justify their argument – that evidence used by Alexander was problematic – by reference to their earlier criticism of the ORACLE study (Scarth and Hammersley, 1986, 1987). This criticism, however, did not refer to the forms of classroom organization but concerned styles of questioning within ORACLE and they fail to mention the subsequent research which confirmed the original ORACLE findings. By their own standards, therefore, Hammersley and Scarth (1993) are far from convincing when questioning the quality of the evidence on classroom organization presented in this section of the 'Three Wise Men's' report.

However, these two critics are on stronger ground when claiming that these classroom data have been misinterpreted. One suspects that, whereas the task of summarizing the research evidence was left to Alexander as the academic member of the team, the interpretation of this evidence relied heavily on HMI preconceptions, based upon inspection reports, mixed with the views of the third 'Wise Man', similar to the ones displayed in his *Guardian* statement. Interestingly, to back up this speculation, much of the evidence used in this section to support these conclusions is taken from HMI reports and not directly from the research. Thus, the conclusion that planning has improved as a result of the National Curriculum (para 58) is based on HMI surveys and the criticism of topics and the preference for single-subject study again depends upon HMI conclusions (paras 67–72). There is no reference to the work of Mortimore *et al.* (1988) or Galton and Patrick (1990) who both come to the same conclusions that topic work, in the form described by HMI, is infrequently used. Both sets of researchers demonstrate that, for the most part, primary teachers rarely combined more than two subjects into any activity, having learnt from practice that increasing the number of subjects beyond this made their task unmanageable. Maintaining an argument that primary schools were 'awash' with interdisciplinary topics is, however, crucial to the case for a greater degree of specialization since, when teaching topics in this way, curricular expertise of such a level is required that 'it makes impossible demands on the subject knowledge of the general primary teacher' (para 77). Evidence of particular failures in the Leeds Primary Needs Project can then be used to support the claim that subject specialist teachers are required, rather than continuing with class teachers and making use of subject coordinators to improve these 'generalist's' practice (paras 78–80).

Having advocated a move to specialized teaching, particularly in the junior school, the organization of such classes then poses problems for the 'Three Wise Men'. While rejecting streaming (paras 84–5), they come down in favour of differentiation by grouping within the class, regarding 'this as a sensible strategy' (para 85). There is, however, no penetrating discussion, as in Hart (1992), of what this concept of differentiation might involve. Instead, the language used becomes reminiscent of the earlier *Framework for the Primary Curriculum* discussed in Chapter 2, particularly when passages relate to aspects of classroom practice. Conclusions become fuzzy and qualifications abound so that, for example, having just argued that grouping by ability is a sensible strategy, the report then refers to 'the mounting evidence about teacher under-expectation and pupil under-achievement which means, however, that teachers must avoid the pitfalls of assuming that the pupils' ability is fixed' (para 65). How such expectations can be avoided, once grouping by ability or setting has been legitimated, is not adequately discussed.

On the different organizational strategies, the report relies heavily on the research evidence concerning individual teaching and the fact that the interaction between teachers and pupils is often superficial, brief and infrequent (para 88). From this the report moves towards support for whole-class teaching on the grounds that it is 'associated with higher order questioning, explanations and statements and these in turn correlate with pupil performance' (para 90). The 'Three Wise Men', however, do go on to point out some of the weaknesses of whole-class teaching (para 91), including reference to the ORACLE studies where pupils were observed to operate a strategy which was termed 'easy riding'. These pupils slowed down their rate of working 'to meet the teacher's norm thus narrowing the challenge of what is taught' (para 91). There is no reference in this section, however, to one of the other important disadvantages of whole-class teaching, namely that most of the children remain silent and listen rather than participate (Galton *et al.*, 1980).

The sections on group work (paras 93–8) rely heavily on the research of Galton and Williamson (1992) and of Bennett and Dunne (1992). The report advises that group work may become counter-productive 'if teachers try to manage too many groups of pupils within the same class or have pupils working on too many activities or subjects simultaneously' (para 97). The conclusion from this section is that it makes good sense to use a mixture of these organizational strategies, as most teachers would already claim to do. However, the key question: when is it most appropriate to use a particular organization, is answered only in the most general terms. The report becomes imprecise in its attempt to indicate to teachers how this mix might be determined. The paragraph uses 'HMI-speak', such as 'fitness for purpose' (para 101) arguing that the teacher must be clear about the goals of learning before deciding on the methods of organization. However, these goals are not elaborated. More importantly, neither is the relationship between the different task demands which arise from these goals and the different teaching strategies considered. Later, the importance of teachers 'being competent in a range of techniques in order to achieve different learning outcomes' (para 103) is stated but, again, there is no discussion of the relationship between these learning outcomes and these techniques. Further, in this section the report introduces the notion of *direct* and *indirect* teaching but nowhere clearly defines these constructs. There is an implication that direct teaching involves little more than pupils being told things and teachers pointing out to pupils when they are in the wrong (p104). At no point is *direct teaching* contrasted with *direct instruction*, the term used by researchers.

It is at this point that Hammersley and Scarth's (1993) claim that the 'Three Wise Men' went beyond the evidence understates their case. The report offers no serious research evidence to back up its claims that 'there are persistent and damaging beliefs' that pupils 'should never be told things only ask questions' and that teachers 'must never point out when a pupil is wrong since to proffer anything but unqualified praise and the child's confidence will be undermined for ever' (p.104). The claims that such practices were widespread, first voiced by the 'Black Paper' writers in the late 1970s, were thoroughly investigated and refuted during the ORACLE studies (Galton *et al.,* 1980). The rhetoric adopted here sits uneasily with the more serious analysis of the previous paragraph. In the final parts of the report, when dealing with assessing and recording progress, there is a reference to giving *genuine feedback* (para 115) but the resulting discussion is woefully thin and ignores the crucial distinction between *critical* and *evaluative* feedback (Galton and Williamson, 1992, pp.96–7).

A careful reading of the report suggests, therefore, that there was a debate between the three participants about placing the evidence collected within different contexts. As the chief executive of the National Curriculum Council, Chris Woodhead would have been committed to his organization's approach to raising standards and, presumably, anxious to have this view endorsed in the report. Thus any implied criticism that the confusion surrounding the implementation of the National Curriculum, of the kind described in the earlier chapters, could have contributed to the current ills of primary schools, would have been difficult to accept. Alexander's plea that 'policy makers' should also look for reasons why primary practice had not improved probably met with resistance. Woodhead's lack of primary experience also naturally inclined him towards a secondary school approach; with greater emphasis on whole-class 'specialist subject' teaching, less topic work, more testing and assessing and, by implication, greater disciplinary control. This view totally ignores the substantial body of research stressing the need to use different teaching approaches for different tasks, particularly when differentiating between the acquisition of *procedural knowledge* and *conceptual knowledge* of the kind required for complex problem-solving, and neglects any consideration of the wide uses of *direct instruction*. Instead, the cruder term, *direct teaching* is used throughout the report, allowing ministers to interpret the findings as a call for a return to 'basics'. For example, many of the same issues were subsequently picked out by the then Secretary of State, Kenneth Clarke, as key 'bullet points' in his press interview (Simon, 1993).

The second context in which efforts were made to situate the report arises out of an HMI perspective: that the weaknesses in primary practice that were observed and reported on by Her Majesty's Inspectorate stemmed largely from teachers' ignorance of the subject matter. As teachers improved their knowledge base, their confidence would increase and they would be prepared to be more flexible in their use of teaching strategies. Teachers would not only present the subjects in more interesting ways but would better understand and correct pupils' learning difficulties. Rose's personal view may well have been influenced by his own scientific training, but also from a reading, or perhaps a misreading, of the debate about the relationship between subject knowledge and pedagogic expertise initiated in the United States by Lee Shulman (1986). (The issue of subject expertise will be considered in the final chapter.) Between Woodhead and Rose, therefore, there was a certain degree of overlap in the way they approached their task when attempting to draw inferences from the various sources of evidence.

The remaining author, Professor Alexander, who had recorded, publicly, his appreciation of the way primary teachers willingly contributed to his work, presumably attempted to limit any potential damage to their morale from some of the report's more critical comments. At the same time he, no doubt, hoped to widen the ongoing debate about the links between subject expertise and pedagogy. In his *Guardian* letter, responding to the charge of being an 'unwise man', he is at pains to point out, for example, that the report was meant as a discussion paper and that differences between the authors related to its 'context' and its 'implications' (*The Guardian,* 14 February 1992, p.20). Nevertheless, many of the 'Three Wise Men's' conclusions agree closely with those in the Leeds PNP Evaluation Report and can also be found in an expanded form elsewhere (Alexander, 1992). Thus on the need for specialist subject teaching in the top half of the junior school, he finds himself on the side of HMI. In other areas he accurately reflects the continuing debate in primary education concerning the development of mixed teaching strategies but presumably failed to carry through this debate by persuading his co-authors of the importance of distinguishing between direct instruction and direct teaching, a distinction of which he would have been very aware.

More importantly, there is no discussion in the report of the manner in which social factors can influence pupils' learning. Although Andrew Pollard's (1985) work is included in the references, the implications of his analysis are not taken up. Presumably it was felt by at least some of the 'wise men' that a discussion of primary pupils' rights as well as duties went too far! Had such an analysis been included, the rather crude distinctions between praise and criticism found in the report might have taken on a more subtle form. Strangely, for a report that criticizes the undue influence of certain theories of learning on teaching, no other alternative models which might be more useful for teachers are discussed. The report has little to say on a crucial issue concerning class teaching, namely how pupils might be grouped together in order to make this more manageable. Nor does it look very closely into the implications of recent research for group work which appears to support mixed rather than single ability groupings (Bennett and Dunne 1992). Knowing whether this was, in part, because the authors felt this research was unrepresentative, or whether they misinterpreted its significance, or whether, as Hammersley and Scarth (1993) argue, they unintentionally gave greater weight to those findings which matched their own personal agendas, will have to wait until Professor Alexander decides to write a definitive account of what took place during those six weeks when the 'Three Wise Men' met to review the evidence. As Simon (1993) argues, in certain parts the report does, by implication, endorse the ideas of Vygotsky, for which credit must presumably be given to Professor Alexander. But it fails to spell out the implications of these ideas fully. The next chapter will attempt to do just that: to provide this missing part of the report, the part, perhaps, Professor Alexander wished to write but under pressure of time, and for a variety of reasons, was not able to.

Chapter 5
Life after Dearing: Teaching and Learning in the Primary School

This chapter is concerned with pedagogy; what Gage (1985) defined as 'the science of the art of teaching'. Gage justifies this approach by comparing education and medicine. For example, in medicine, research on the links between diet and heart disease has helped improve survival rates. In the same way, Gage believes it is possible to learn to teach better by measuring pupil progress and identifying differences between teachers who consistently obtain above average and below average results. However, just as in medicine, where success or failure is ultimately decided by the personal skill of the individual doctor, so too in education the effectiveness of a teaching approach relies on the way the teacher applies this empirical knowledge. In Britain, for a variety of reasons, we have tended to ignore this view of pedagogy which seeks to 'establish general principles of teaching, and, in the light of these, to determine what modifications of practice are needed to meet individual specific needs' (Simon, 1981b, p.141). Lamenting on this lack of interest, Simon concluded that there was so much 'confusion of thought' and disparity of views, that 'to resuscitate the concept of a science of teaching which underlines that of pedagogy may seem to be crying for the moon' (Simon 1981b, p.125).

Over a decade later, writing with a freedom presumably denied him in the 'Three Wise Men's' report, Alexander, in seeking to define 'good primary practice', noted a disparity in the way the term is used by the Plowden Committee (1967) (where it comes closest to both Gage's and Simon's interpretation) and by HMI and by teachers. In seeking to clarify this different usage, Alexander (1993, p.184) has categorized practice under four aspects: content, context, pedagogy and management. Each aspect promotes its own central questions, the answers to which are underpinned by certain ideas, values and beliefs. The debate about content, for example, has to do with ways in which knowledge is presented, whether as an integrated whole or as separate subject areas. Such questions become more important when attempts are made to differentiate between different kinds of knowledge, something lacking in much of the National Curriculum debate. When this is done, then the selection of content impinges on questions of pedagogy, since the central educational questions are concerned not only with what pupils should learn but how best this particular form of knowledge can be presented to children. This statement implies that adopting mixed approaches rather than a single strategy will best serve the teacher's purpose, although it still remains to select the appropriate strategy for the set task.

The context aspect of practice has to do with the physical conditions within the classroom and the ethos (mainly determined by the interpersonal relationships between the teacher and the pupils), while management has to do with such matters as planning and quality assurance through the assessment of learning and the evaluation of teaching. Alexander (1993, p.184) suggests that, since the late 1970s, HMI has consistently tended to define good practice mainly in terms of the content and the management of the curriculum. This view explains why so much advice on good practice, including the 'Three Wise Men's' report, tends to consist of bland 'fuzzy' statements, using catch-all phrases such as 'fitness for purpose'. On the other hand, the National Curriculum approach, while similar to HMI's, tends to emphasize, for reasons that we have seen, planning and assessment. This accords with their mistaken belief that assessment can drive pedagogy in the desired direction. Teachers tend to emphasize the classroom context more than other groups, while also referring to pedagogy in broad terms such as 'formal' and 'informal'. To give a specific example, the physical context is often used to analyse problems of indiscipline in the classroom, on the grounds that if the pupils were involved in interesting activities, in a *well-organized stimulating environment,* they would work more efficiently since there would be *no time or inclination to misbehave.*

As one moves away from Gage's and Simon's concept of pedagogy the rhetoric used to advance alternative prescriptions of 'good practice' becomes more strident in tone and intolerant of other viewpoints. In particular, 'Plowdenism' has now become synonymous with all that is wrong with primary education. Before going further, therefore, it is important to look briefly again at the context within which the Plowden Report was produced. So much has been written about the report, and so many claims made on all sides about why it made or did not make certain recommendations, that it is, perhaps, necessary to be reminded of the initial aims of those who sat down to discuss primary education in the mid-1960s and the context in which these discussions took place.

The Birth of Plowdenism

In the new year edition of *Picture Post* in 1941, at what is generally acknowledged as one of the darkest moments in British history, the Master of Balliol, A. D. Lindsey, produced 'A Plan for Education'. The caption picture above the article in which the plan was discussed showed two boys standing outside Lord's Cricket Ground, dressed in their Eton suits. Next to them were three children in short trousers and open-neck shirts, standing bare-headed and staring at the two public school boys with some amusement. The caption above the picture read, 'Between the two groups is a barrier, deliberately created by our system of education. Our task is to remove that barrier'. In the article, Lindsey went on to argue that,

> there is still on the whole, one system of education for the poor and another for the rich. The conditions under which boys from primary school can climb the educational ladder to the Universities are such that we are praying for a great blessing, democracy in the Universities with a new curse, the production of an intelligencia in the worst sense of the term.

Today, this quotation, if uttered in the House of Commons, would probably be greeted with greater derision than at the time it was written. Lindsey's remarks, particularly the need to sweep away the old system and replace it with something new, became a shared objective on both sides of the House. It led to R. A. Butler's 1944 Education Act, which established universal education for all, although still within a highly selective system with the 11-plus examination and grammar and secondary modern schools. Over the next two decades, evidence continued to mount concerning the ineffectiveness of this selection procedure and, in particular, the rigid streaming process on which it depended. Among this evidence was the sociological research showing the strong links between selection and social class, and the early participant observation studies emanating from the University of Manchester, showing how selection disadvantaged working-class children in both secondary modern and grammar schools. More than these studies, however, the evidence of 'a wastage in ability' emerging from the government's own commissioned surveys helped maintain a degree of consensus about the need for further change. One result was the setting up of a committee by the Conservative education minister, Sir Edward Boyle, to consider the future of primary education.

By the time this committee began its work, the educational climate was moving towards what in Chapter 1 was termed 'reconstructionism', with its associated belief that it was possible to bring about changes in society through education. What spurred the reformers on was a recognition, even then, that with the loss of its empire Britain required a skilled and articulate labour force for its economic survival. This, as much as egalitarian principles, was the spur to reform. Thirty years on, the failure to fulfil these aspirations is now generally acknowledged. Simon (1990, p.9) for example, notes Claus Moser's pessimistic conclusion that 'Britain was in danger of becoming one of the least adequately educated of all advanced nations'. Only in the last few years have the numbers entering university increased appreciably but this has happened in a period when resources have declined and there is still a major shortage of well-trained, skilled workers.

It is necessary to provide this résumé given that during the last few years both major political parties have called for the reintroduction of streaming in top junior classes. When the Plowden Committee first met, streaming was still a controversial issue. The Committee, while recognizing the damage that the existing system caused, had no ready-made alternative organizational arrangement which they could recommend to teachers with mixed ability classes. Elsewhere Galton (1989) has argued that it was the changes at secondary level, resulting in the growth of comprehensive schools and the consequent redundancy of the 11-plus, which promoted the greatest change in practice, because teachers now had to find ways of coping with heterogeneous groups. Teachers' responses were pragmatic ones, for example, the use of curricula groups. In the ORACLE study this approach described a style of teaching called 'rotating changers' where either pupils moved to and from different curriculum tables or stayed at the same table but changed their topic at regular intervals (Galton *et al.*, 1980). This style, however, was never a popular one because of the time wasted during changeovers. Only 15 per cent of the ORACLE sample made frequent use of it. Gradually, as more recent studies showed, the strategy was abandoned and the number of subjects 'on the go' at any time during topic work was generally limited to two. This kind of practical experimentation probably went on for at least five years after the Plowden Committee had reported.

It is important to stress this element of experimentation because some of the more extreme rhetoric emanating from the 1970 Black Paper writers such as Timothy Raison has remained a part of the 'folk law' concerning the alleged damage done to primary education by 'Plowdenism'. This could be seen in the previous chapter where 'echoes' of that same rhetoric were to be found in the 'Three Wise Men's' report. In reality, subsequent research suggests that after Plowden, most teachers decided, mainly on pragmatic grounds, to use a mix of organizational methods. Decisions about which method to use on different occasions were made according to what is now termed 'fitness for purpose'. Taken at its fullest, 'fitness for purpose' should presumably mean that teachers would identify the type of knowledge required to complete the tasks they set the pupils, would then identify the learning processes involved in acquiring this knowledge and would then choose a teaching methodology which matched these learning requirements.

However, the 'Three Wise Men's' report (para 101) – where in deciding on methods of organization the 'critical notion' is said to be 'fitness for purpose' – nowhere discusses the relationship between types of knowledge, learning demands and teaching strategies. The 'Three Wise Men' do, it is true, refer to the 'goals of learning' but in a context which suggests that they mean nothing more than a 'statement of attainment'. 'Fitness for purpose', therefore, probably means no more now than in the immediate post-Plowden period, namely that a teacher should look at what the task demands of pupils and then decide how best this might be organized according to the composition of the class and the resources required. The survival of this approach in curriculum decision making for nearly 30 years is not altogether surprising, given that yesterday's Plowden teachers became today's senior advisers and inspectors (including one of the 'Three Wise Men').

Viewed in this way, 'fitness for purpose' explains the strong emphasis on individualization which developed in the post-Plowden era. There were wide variations in the amount of work being done by different pupils in subjects such as English and mathematics (partly because of the range of ability within the class but also, as was pointed out in Chapter 1, because the lack of motivation for these tasks on the part of some pupils gave rise to avoidance strategies such as 'easy riding' and 'intermittent working'). Teachers therefore decided that such lessons were best introduced either to the whole class or to a group, and then continued through schemes involving books and worksheets which pupils worked through at their own pace. This pattern has largely continued to the present day. History topics, on the other hand, could often be taught to the whole class. Teachers could tell stories about the past and then follow this with group activities where children created materials for display using information from resource packs or books. Similar patterns were developed for science, which mainly consisted of studying natural phenomena (what in an earlier epoch was timetabled as 'nature study'). Within such arrangements teachers had to find alternative tasks which some children could do without requiring help. This allowed the teacher time to instruct the groups. For these reasons, the patterns of classroom organization in primary classrooms probably closely reflected the proportions of time allocated to different subject areas of the curriculum until well into the mid-1980s.

Two decades earlier, however, the Plowden Committee had needed to justify the shift from the normal ' secondary school' pattern of organization associated with streaming. At the time, evidence for shifting the balance of organization away from class teaching was to hand in the form of the discoveries made by Piaget and his colleagues, particularly the work on language acquisition and on the conservation of number. Piaget's ideas will be discussed later in the chapter but here it need only be said, as pointed out by Alexander (1993), that these theories fitted well with a number of other reform movements, most importantly, the arts and crafts movement developed by Robin Tanner, who as an HMI worked for a considerable period in the Oxfordshire area. When all these strands were combined, particularly that emanating from Tanner with its focus on integration of knowledge, the portrait of a Plowden classroom described by Simon (1981a) can be seen to possess a logical justification. But since, as Chapter 1 attempted to demonstrate, the implementation of curriculum change is not a rational process, it was never to be expected that this 'Plowden classroom' would be widely adopted. Simon (1981a) estimated that only about 10 per cent of the primary teaching population could be said to have embraced the 'Plowden' style at the time the report was published, and that nothing much had changed by 1970 when the ORACLE research began.

There were two important reasons for this resistance to change. First, the proposed changes conflicted with what appears to be a very stable characteristic of teaching, known, after the researcher who formulated it, as the 'Flander's two-thirds rule'. This rule states that, for two-thirds of the time, there is talk going on in the classroom and that the teacher is doing two-thirds of this talking (Flanders, 1964). Teachers find it difficult to shift from a pattern where they provide most of the information and ask questions, to one where they listen to the pupils and encourage the children to offer up their own ideas for discussion. The second reason why most teachers did not fully adopt the Plowden methodology was a consequence of this determination by teachers to remain the major resource in the classroom. Attending to the individual requirements of upwards of 30 children made impossible demands on teachers. This was demonstrated during the ORACLE studies (Galton *et al.,* 1980) where only some 10 per cent adopted an approach which resembled the 'Plowden' style. These teachers interacted with pupils for over 90 per cent of the day compared to an average of 70 per cent for most teachers. Given this fact, other kinds of work required of teachers, including preparation, marking and setting up displays, had to be done after school hours. Teachers who adopted this approach, such as those observed by Galton (1989), worked a ten-hour day, coming into school at 8 in the morning and going home at 6 in the evening.

One major success of Plowden, however, was that, perhaps for the first time in this country, it caused primary teaching to become the subject of serious intellectual enquiry. By its arguments and its recourse to research evidence, it clearly demonstrated that primary teachers required not only practical skills but well-trained lively enquiring minds, and this fact led indirectly to the establishment of four-year B.Ed. degrees. What Plowden could not have anticipated, however, were the enormous social changes during the next two decades which would affect the nature of relationships between teachers and pupils, even pupils as young as those entering first school. This was, in part, a consequence of Piagetian theory which gave a low priority to these social factors in its model of child development. One key change since the early 1960s has been the dramatic way in which our respect for 'institutional' authority has declined. Teaching methods have been slow to adapt to this change in attitudes with a result, as Galton (1989) has argued, that there is now a disjuncture between the way pupils are expected to learn and the way they are expected to behave in the class-room. To cope with this problem many pupils adopt a strategy of dependency to avoid participating in class until they are certain of the intention behind the teacher's requests. This puts more pressure on the teacher, making it impossible to offer help to individual pupils in the manner of a one-to-one university seminar (Simon, 1981a). Neither Plowden nor others within education could have anticipated these problems at the time the report was produced.

Returning to today's schools, headteachers, as the Leeds PNP evaluation demonstrated (Alexander, 1991), seek to justify what goes on in their schools by means of both conceptual and value perspectives. Alexander found these perspectives relied heavily on 'Plowdenism' and bore little relationship to observed practice. Looking back to the immediate aftermath of the report it becomes possible to offer an explanation as to how this gulf between 'rhetoric' and 'reality' may have developed. Headteachers needed to justify the practices adopted by their teachers to deal with the problems of mixed ability teaching once the practice of streaming ended. Plowden was readily available as part of this justification. In time, some of these headteachers moved either into colleges of education or into the advisory services and even the inspectorate. Added to this, during the development of the B.Ed, large numbers of non-primary specialists were recruited into colleges of education to teach the subject elements of the primary curriculum. Many of these acquired an additional qualification in the educational disciplines so that those teaching educational theory within the colleges also lacked any practical primary experience. That theorizing went on cannot be denied. That it was highly influential in determing practice must be disputed. Post-Plowden 'hybrid' practice has, from the evidence of all the research studies, remained relatively stable in most primary schools over the last 20 years. A case can, therefore, be made that these accepted weaknesses, well-documented since the late 1970s, are not mainly due to the influence of any theories of progressivism but can be more convincingly attributed to the failure of bodies such as HMI, teacher trainers, LEA advisers and, more recently, the National Curriculum Council, to engage intellectually with the concept of pedagogy and to define clearly the terms which they so freely used when proffering advice to teachers on good practice. Chief among these undefined terms is that of 'fitness for purpose'.

The Need for Theories

Despite this evidence to the contrary, part of the government's recent complaints about LEAs and university departments of education has been that they have forced teachers to adopt practices based upon uncritical interpretations of child development theory. The National Curriculum Council, for its part, appears to have been staffed at senior level with people who have also placed little faith in such theorizing (presumably, if they had espoused the alternative point of view they would not have been appointed by the Secretary of State for Education in the first place!). There are also those in education who would support this position. For example, in a recent book, David McNamara (1994) has argued that teaching is a 'common sense' activity, highly developed even in young children. He cites the case of his own daughter whom he observed teaching her dolls to add. She tells her father that in the afternoon the dolls are going to learn 'take aways'. When her father asks her how she knows the dolls are ready for this change, she replies that she had given them a test and they got 20 out of 25. For McNamara the basic processes of teaching (explanation, followed by practice then testing and, if necessary, recapitulation) are all present within this episode. All that is required of the teacher is a mastery of the necessary subject matter knowledge and an ability to communicate this subject matter in a manner whereby it is readily understood by the pupils. In Professor McNamara's opinion, the contribution of psychology, and in particular, developmental psychology, to this process is negligible. His argument is as follows:

> Since it has been claimed that developmental psychology is characterised by ignorance about the very processes of development, and that it is in precisely this area where the practitioner would need information in order to optimise children's learning that it is at its most deficient, one wonders why educationalists continue to press its claims. Psychologists have, at various times, attempted to remind educationalists that psychology was an academic discipline which is distinguished by debate and controversy about what it actually knows, with competing schools of thought offering alternative inter-pretations and accounts of the mind and its functioning, and that even if psychological knowledge was in some sense 'fact' or 'true' it would not translate readily into classroom practice. (McNamara, 1994, p.27)

Of course, McNamara is right to insist that theory, of whatever kind, cannot be used prescriptively to determine strategies for teaching. At its best, because, as he again rightly points out, there will always be uncer-tainty and conflicting explanations, psychological theory can only be used as a working hypothesis to help teachers' check on their own prac-tical solutions to classroom problems, particularly those concerning the pupils' learning difficulties. It is doubtful, however, whether teachers have ever taken a position where they have allowed theory, in whatever guise, to completely overrule the common sense approach.

However, there are also good reasons for rejecting the notion that pedagogy can be based solely on this 'common sense' approach (or on what has come to be known as teachers' 'craft knowledge'). Clearly this professional expertise must form a part of any 'science of the art of teaching' but the teacher's view of classroom events is only a partial one because of what Galton (1989) has called the 'perception gap'. This leads teachers to block out certain events in the classroom which might cause discomfort, particularly those that might cause colleagues to conclude that the teacher was not competent. Galton (1989) describes such an occasion when he shouted at pupils and banged the table while demanding the return of a set of needles which were needed for sewing. He had previously been requested by another teacher to 'make certain that all the needles with large eyes were returned'. Proving himself to be a good teacher required him to be able to say to his colleague on her return, 'You gave me ten needles. I'm returning all ten'. This partial view of classroom events, particularly since it tends to 'gloss over' less than satisfactory occurrences, is clearly not a basis for developing a model of pedagogy. It is not always possible to have a colleague chal-lenge the teacher's own version of events as in Galton's case.

Another reason for regarding theories based solely on teachers' common sense view of practice as inadequate, relates to a second factor which distorts the interpretation of events. This has to do with attribution theory (Weiner, 1986). The theory predicts that where an individual perceives a lack of success, the person involved will tend to attribute the reasons for this failure to factors which lie outside their own immediate personal control. Thus teachers often tend to blame home background or a pupil's character for a poor performance. With group work, for example, many teachers claim that primary-aged pupils 'are not mature enough to cooperate effectively'. External observers, such as classroom researchers, often see events in a different light. In Galton and Williamson (1992) there is an good example of this mechanism at work, where one of the authors observes a year group of lower junior pupils taught by two teachers. It is clear that the observer puts the failures of the lesson down to poor planning and to the way in which control is exercised. On the following afternoon, however, when the researcher has the same class, it is noticeable that in the fieldwork notes most of the blame for similar problems is attributed to the pupils' and not to the teacher's actions. Now the pupils are continually accused of not concentrating, with the researcher, like the two teachers earlier, asking, 'Will you listen?', 'Why don't you listen, why can't you concentrate?' At the end of the episode, the fieldnote concludes:

> We end the day, I suspect on all sides feeling very smug. Me, inwardly, because I think this experience proves my point. There has to be another way of dealing with the children and no doubt both Pat and Mary (*the two teachers*) because they think I now know what it is like to teach these kids and that maybe I will not be so full of theory next time. Mary was working nearby when I had the children lining up to go to the Library and no doubt heard my voice raise in frustration as I asked them for the umpteenth time 'Why don't you listen?' and, indeed, asking Mark the classic question, 'What did I say a moment ago?' with him being unable to tell me. (Galton and Williamson, 1992, p.118)

It should be reasonably clear from the above account that all involved with these children could easily reinforce each other's interpretation of events in ways that supported, for example, the view that the class couldn't cope with working independently in groups. This might justify a continued preference for whole-class teaching, followed by seat work. When seeking to solve the practical problems of teaching 30 lively children within a crowded classroom, both the perception and attribution effects may, therefore, point us towards solutions which suit our needs as teachers. But, since such an analysis rarely looks at the problem from the pupils' perspective, the solution chosen may not be the best one for the children. For a wider perspective we need to take into account other sources of evidence, particularly those which relate to the effects of our teaching upon the pupils. Theory, therefore, is useful not as a prescription but as a way of testing out our own 'common sense' views of what constitutes effective practice.

There is still a problem of which theory to choose since, as McNamara (1994) correctly argues, in an academic discipline such as psychology, there are bound to be a number of alternative explanatory models available at any point in time. But in matters of teaching and learning, knowledge can either come from empirical studies such as the ORACLE research or from experimentation of the kind conducted by a Bruner or a Piaget (Kyriacou, 1986). However, such experiments are generally artificial in the sense that they take place in a laboratory, which usually does not accurately replicate classroom conditions. Experiments therefore lack what is called 'external validity' and as such have to be treated with caution unless backed up by large-scale observational research in 'naturalistic' classroom settings (Rosenshine and Furst, 1973). From this starting point it becomes possible to propose that an effective pedagogical theory must reconcile both experimental theory and naturalistic empirical enquiry with the common sense 'craft knowledge' of the expert teacher. The reason for focusing on experts will become clear when the characteristics of such teachers are described in the next chapter. One particular quality relevant to the present discussion is that they tend, more than their colleagues, to view classroom events from the pupils' perspective as well as their own. If, therefore, all three sources of evidence tend towards similar solutions, then it is not unreasonable to value such practice highly. However, such 'triangulated' theory should still not be treated prescriptively because in classrooms, as in all cases of human activity, there will be variations in behaviour among individuals due to a number of possibly unknown factors. This does not mean that we need to abandon the search for a pedagogy or to base our curriculum planning solely on the needs of the individual. As Simon (1981b) has argued, this latter approach is unworkable and results in the kinds of diversity in practice that led to the call for a National Curriculum. Instead we need to be begin,

> From the opposite standpoint with what the children have in common as members of the human species. To establish the general principles of teaching and, in the light of these, to determine what modifications of practice are needed to meet specific individual needs. (Simon, 1981b, p.141)

Children as Thinkers and Learners

At the time of the Plowden Report, as Wood (1988 p.2) explains, key ideas on children's' learning which were 'neglected for the previous twenty years or so were destined to receive prominence thereafter'. These ideas of Piaget replaced previous theories based upon principles of 'positive reinforcement' because they were able to offer more satisfactory explanations for 'self-directed problem solving' and the observed phenomenon of 'critical periods of learning' (p.5).

Since the 1960s, however, much has been written which is critical of Piagetian ideas and his methodology. Among the criticisms listed by Meadows (1993) are that Piaget underestimated the importance of language, that the children failed to make sense of the questions they were asked in the experiments, and that they did not understand the tasks they were asked to do. Piaget also paid insufficient attention to the social situation, particularly to the relationships between the adult inquisitor and the child. Wood, along with many other contemporary theorists of child development, continues to accept Piaget's view that children actively 'construct' their knowledge of the world (Wood, 1988, p.15) but he departs from ' classical' Piagetian theory at a number of important points, crucially, 'that adults, social interaction and communication play a far more formative role in the development of children's thinking and learning than the theory allows'. 'Children's knowledge is often a product of the joint construction of understanding by the child and by more expert members of his culture' (Wood, 1988, p.60).

When those responsible for training teachers first attempted to apply Piaget's ideas to the classroom they interpreted his findings in a very narrow way. Just as the classical 'humanist' apprenticeship model of teaching regarded children as empty vessels into which teachers poured knowledge, so now, when interpreting Piaget's stage theory, children were thought incapable of thinking in certain ways until a point was reached at which 'the child's own existing understanding, based on his commerce with nature, is in an appropriate state of readiness for change' (Wood, 1988, p.16). This concept of readiness helped to bring a decline of interest in pedagogy because pupils' failures to understand could now be attributed to their stage of development rather than to inappropriate teaching methods (Simon, 1981b).

Over time this view has been modified. It is generally recognized that pupils do have some understanding of concepts which even adults have difficulty in fully comprehending. Meadows (1993, pp.122–3), for example, describes young children's thoughts on health, sickness and death, as well as their attempts at explaining their emotions and people. Bennett (1992) discusses the case of a class of 9-year-old pupils and their ideas of shadows. One-third of the class argued that a shadow was an area blotted out from the sun's rays by an object, whereas another third said that a shadow was caused by the body acting as a mirror which reflects the sun's rays on the floor. One child believed the shadow was a little black thing that followed you about! Such differences present a formidable challenge to teachers who attempt to practise the principle that 'it is better to begin by building on what the child already knows'.

In recent years, therefore, much greater emphasis has been placed on attempting to understand the processes by which a person moves from an incorrect (or partially correct) understanding of a concept to the correct one and the best means to facilitate this transition. One alternative approach for dealing with this problem is through models of 'information processing'. These are reviewed by Meadows (1993, pp.210–35) and are based on the analogy of 'man as a computer'. Like the mind, a digital computer has both short-term and long-term memory stores. It has a central processing unit which makes use of specific procedures and routines to solve particular problems, with the choice of the appropriate routine governed by a system of 'executive control'. Many problems in computing are solved by a process of approximation and iteration where the first attempt is a guess (perhaps based on previous experience). The guess is used for an initial calculation and the result fed back into the program to provide a better solution. The result of this second calculation is again put back into the system and this process goes on until very little improvement can be detected in successive solutions. This process of 'construction' and 'reconstruction' clearly has parallels with a view of thinking as 'restructuring' and 'tuning'.

Meadows (1993, p.214), in her review of the literature, notes that many of the general cognitive theories of information processing do not sufficiently distinguish between different task demands nor on the kind of knowledge to be acquired. What children do is constrained by their own cognitive limitations, but it is also directed by what they think the task requires. Meadows therefore argues that an analysis of the task's demands is vital, particularly 'how tasks and learners change with practice' (p.224). Another Alexander, this time Patricia, has made a similar point (Alexander et al., 1991). They examined the writings of researchers on learning and identified at least 13 undifferentiated uses of the word 'knowledge'. These are listed in Table 5.1.

Meadows concludes that information-processing models of cognitive development, as opposed to the 'very basic studies and processes which involve all cognitive functioning', have limited application for teachers.

Rather than continue with the metaphor of the 'man as computer' she argues that more attention should be paid to biological theories which view 'minds as brains' (p.219). However, the computer model seems useful for understanding how declarative, procedural and strategic

Table 5.1 Some definitions of knowledge

CONCEPTUAL KNOWLEDGE: Knowledge of ideas. How they function and the conditions when they should be used.

CONDITIONAL KNOWLEDGE: Where knowledge should (or could) be applied.

CONTENT KNOWLEDGE: Knowledge of some aspect of the mental, physical or social world.

DECLARATIVE KNOWLEDGE: Factual information ('knowing what').

DISCIPLINE KNOWLEDGE: A specialised field or branch of learning.

DISCOURSE KNOWLEDGE: Knowledge of language and its use.

DOMAIN KNOWLEDGE: Subset of Content Knowledge.

METACOGNITIVE KNOWLEDGE: Knowledge of knowledge, cognition and the regulation of cognition.

PRIOR KNOWLEDGE: Sum of what an individual already knows.

PROCEDURAL KNOWLEDGE: Knowledge of routines ('knowing how').

SCHEMA KNOWLEDGE: Knowledge represented in structures which are embedded in one another.

STRATEGIC KNOWLEDGE: Knowledge of processes for knowledge acquisition.

TASK KNOWLEDGE: An understanding of the cognitive demands of a task.

Taken from Alexander, P. et al. (1991)

knowledge can be acquired and used in solving problems where there is a correct or preferred answer. It seems less helpful in explaining how prior knowledge and metacognitive processes interact when pupils attempt to solve more complex open-ended problems.

Observation in primary classes (Galton, 1989) suggests that many teachers could benefit from using the computer model when, for example, setting a practical task in science requiring the application of data-gathering procedures, data manipulation and problem-solving. Junior school pupils often approached such problems in what teachers referred to as a 'undisciplined way' because they lacked the necessary manipulative skills, procedures and routines to obtain consistent data, or the capacity to present the information in ways which related to the problem to be solved. To test this out, a class was asked to time two 'beeps' on a tape recording separated by an interval of 25 seconds. The range of times recorded varied from 15 seconds to 3 minutes! Although these pupils had all done experiments in which a stopwatch had been required, none had systematically practised using a stopwatch so that the procedures involved became automatic and the results consistent. Other strategies such as 'chunking' factual information into larger units so that it is easier for encoding, storage and retrieval are also clearly appropriate in teaching. Perhaps of even greater importance is the need to teach children self-regulating mechanisms such as collecting 'feedback' information when deciding whether to accept or reject a solution to a problem.

Pintrich and his colleagues, who make the latter suggestion, also support Meadows when arguing that information-processing models do not explain why pupils 'who seem to have the requisite prior conceptual knowledge do not activate this for many school tasks'. These researchers believe that 'classroom contextual factors' as well as a student's 'motivational beliefs' also determine their 'level of engagement and willingness to persist at a task' (Pintrich *et al.*, 1993, pp.167–8). Here the ideas associated with the Russian psychologist, Vygotsky, assume greater importance, particularly when the prior conceptual knowledge is only partial. For Meadows (1993, p.236), the essential distinction between Vygotsky and either Piagetian or information-processing approaches is that the latter theories attempt to explain behaviour in ways which are 'invariant across cultures'. The acquisition of new knowledge involves some internal process which constructs 'an internal model of outside reality'. Vygotskian theory, on the other hand, regards these models as formed and built up in part by social phenomena so that they are public and inter-subjective, created through interaction with the social environment. Acquisition of cognitive development in these terms therefore 'involves the interaction, transformation and use of routines, ideas and skills which are learned socially from more competent partners' (Meadows, 1993, p.238). Wood makes the same point in defining readiness in Vygotskian terms as 'the capacity of the child to learn with help' (Wood, 1988, p.25).

The most frequently mentioned of Vygotsky's ideas is the zone of proximal development (ZPD). This refers to the 'gap that exists for an individual child between what he is able to do alone and what he can achieve with help from one more knowledgeable and skilled than himself' (Wood, 1988, p.25). The lower point of the zone is marked by what the child can do unaided, while the upper end denotes what he or she can do with appropriate help from the teacher or a more competent peer. In crossing the ZPD, therefore, there is a change from *other-regulation* (peer or adult) to *self-regulation* (Brown and Palincsar, 1986). A crucial question, therefore, is how one can help the individual to complete this passage successfully. Here, Wood (1988, p.25) argues, Vygotsky's ideas come very close to those of Bruner who sees the teacher or more competent peers as 'vicars of culture'. Meadows (1993, p.248) emphasizes the same point, quoting Bruner's own explanation of this role as serving,

> the learner as a vicarious form of consciousness until such a time as the learner is able to master his own actions through his own consciousness and control. When the child achieves that conscious control over a new function or conceptual system, it is then he is able to use it as a tool. Up to that point, the tutor, in effect, performs the critical function of 'scaffolding' the learning tasks to make it possible for the child, in Vygotsky's words, to internalise external knowledge and convert it to a tool for conscious control. (Bruner, 1985, p.25)

Summing up, Wood (1988, p.36) argues that Bruner seems to stand in some way as a link between Piaget and Vygotsky. Bruner shares with Piaget the emphasis on the importance of evolutionary process on the development of the human mind but, at the same time, like Vygotsky, he stresses the influence of the way in which culture forms and can transform this process of development. Thus Bruner gives a more central role than Piaget does to social interaction, while opening up a debate about how children with 'possibly weak preparation can still engage in intellectually challenging problem solving, given the provision of adequate supporting scaffolding' (Resnick and Collins, 1994, p.836).

What has Learning Theory to do with Teaching?

Given these different explanations of the ways in which children learn to think, it would appear that McNamara (1994) has a valid point when questioning the use of such theory in teaching. However, the theories become more useful when set alongside the findings from empirical observational studies of teaching. Together, theory and empirical enquiry can be used to provide the kind of guidance on pedagogy which was lacking in the 'Three Wise Men's' report. This guidance can then be validated by seeking the views of teachers who are acknowledged by their peers to be experts in the particular aspect of teaching the curriculum.

During the 1980s, a considerable proportion of the empirical research carried out in primary classrooms focused on the effectiveness of what came to be known as 'direct instruction' procedures in teaching. These researchers insisted on making a clear distinction between this process and that of 'direct teaching' because they were dissatisfied with the way the latter term was defined by Flanders (1964) who had contrasted it with 'indirect teaching'. 'Direct' teachers were those who lectured, asked questions and were cautious in their use of praise, in contrast to 'Indirect' ones who encouraged pupils to ask questions and to express their ideas and feelings within a warm, friendly classroom atmosphere. Clearly, this was the distinction in mind when, as quoted in the previous chapter, the author of the passage in the 'The Wise Men's' report referred to teachers who never 'proffer anything but unqualified praise' and to the 'persistent and damaging belief that pupils should never be told things, only asked questions' (Alexander *et al.*, 1992, para 104). Towards the end of the paragraph the report specifically calls for the balance between 'direct' and 'indirect' teaching to be reviewed.

Those responsible for developing the idea of direct instruction, however, regarded this dichotomy as a false one. They were particularly anxious that direct instruction should not be equated with a 'back to basics movement' where pupils 'sat in straight rows of desks' and 'spent long periods on academic drills' (Denham and Liberman, 1980, p.288). According to these researchers, it should be perfectly possible for teachers to provide information and ask questions, while at the same time giving praise and providing a generally supportive ethos (Rosenshine, 1979). Another important component of this form of teaching, not emphasized by those using the term 'direct teaching', is in the use made of feedback. Here, unlike in the 'Three Wise Men's' report, feedback does not simply involve showing pupils where they are wrong and correcting their mistakes – what Galton (1989) terms 'evaluative' feedback. In addition, given the importance that direct instruction places on the effective use of class time, pupils should also be taught to use feedback so that while 'on task' they become self-regulating and can work without frequently needing the teacher's help.

This form of 'critical' feedback has more to do with the use of 'scaffolding' which Brown and Palincsar (1986, p.36) define as an 'adjustable and temporary support that can be removed when no longer necessary'. One example they give is the use of 'cue cards' for describing an object. The card would remind pupils to deal with aspects such as colour, shape and size but would also pose questions such as, 'What is the most interesting feature?'. In this instance, feedback involves questioning the pupils' ideas and clarifying their responses; at other times it might involve summarizing and predicting. This is a far cry from the situation where the teacher tells the pupil that they have a wrong answer and then proceeds to explain how to get the correct one. Here the purpose of feedback is to provide the pupil with a means of monitoring his or her progress by noting the points of agreement or disagreement with the instructor (be it the teacher or a more competent peer). In this role the teacher acts not in the capacity of a judge as to the correctness or incorrectness of the pupil's response but as someone offering friendly criticism. Brown and Palincsar (1986) use the term 'reciprocal teaching' to indicate the practice of these critical evaluative strategies.

In its most extreme form, direct instruction involves regular use of a set of standard procedures. The lesson should begin with a brief recapitulation of what was learnt on the previous occasion, followed by a short practice to see if the essential information or skill has been retained. This is then followed by the introduction of new ideas and then further practice. The lesson is concluded by rewarding the class for successful completion of the task (a game, or a quiz is usually suggested by the American researchers). Homework is also an important part of the process, provided that the homework is directed towards the individual pupil's need and is not a general class activity. Apart from reading, this kind of homework is not a regular feature of British primary classrooms. When homework is tailored to individual needs it contributes to another key determinant of success in the direct instruction model: the time pupils spend 'on task'. This variable is directly proportional to the level of achievement, provided that the instruction is appropriately matched. It follows, therefore, that with limited time available in school for each subject, pupils who are experiencing difficulties can catch up if appropriate homework is set.

However, in summarizing the research evidence on direct instruction, Rosenshine (1987) is very clear that its demonstrated success largely involves the acquisition of what, in Table 5.1, was termed 'content, declarative and procedural knowledge'. More complex operations involving, for example, the acquisition of conceptual knowledge and metacognitive knowledge are less amenable to this kind of teaching. This suggests that ideas to do with the 'man as a computer' model, in its less sophisticated applications to do with general cognitive functioning, can be useful in focusing our attention on key aspects of the learning process during direct instruction. With children of primary age, therefore, direct instruction is best used in the acquisition of the kinds of competences associated with 'the basic skills'. Children taught as a class tend to make the greatest progress in these 'basics', not because class teaching has some special intrinsic merit but because, as Brophy and Good (1986) argue, it makes the most efficient use of the teacher's and pupils' time. When the differences in pupils' comprehension is large, as is generally true of mixed-age classes, opportunities for a general presentation are more limited. The next best thing is clearly to group children who are at similar stages together (i.e., ability grouping) and to instruct each group in turn. Most teachers already use such groups for English and mathematics, where instruction followed by seat work is the norm.

This leaves the more difficult problem of helping children acquire more complex forms of knowledge, which do not appear from the empirical evidence to be amenable to direct instruction. Here, the model of cognitive development based upon Vygotsky's ideas appears more appropriate, that is, a model based on cooperative learning. Given one teacher and 30 pupils, such groups will often need to rely on the use of more competent peers to provide the necessary 'scaffolding' for those children who have yet to acquire a particular concept. Indeed, one may infer from Vygotsky that, at times, this may be the preferable procedure because the language of the more competent pupil may be easier for the others in the group to understand. For example, the more competent peers' recent experience of coming to understand how shadows are formed (Bennett, 1992) may speak more directly to other children with only a partial understanding of the concept. The available evidence (Bennett and Dunne, 1992; Slavin, 1986) supports the principle that cooperative groups must contain at least one high ability pupil. In Bennett's study, the quality of the dialogue (judged on the number of correct explanations) was poorer when groups were not of mixed ability. These findings do not therefore support the calls by politicians of both major political parties for streaming and banding at the top end of the junior school. The kinds of tasks that are suitable for this peer tutoring approach will be those such as writing original stories, developing hypotheses in science, understanding and evaluating historical evidence, as well as the application of mathematical procedures to problems demanding abstract reasoning.

There still remains the question of individualization where, as Piaget argued, the child learns best through interacting with the surrounding environment. Teachers are no longer directly involved other than to facilitate this process. Here, Brown and Palincsar (1986, pp.34–5) argue that it is a mistake to see Piaget's theory of child development in direct opposition to that of Vygotsky. Instead, the two theories should be seen as the ends of a continuum. By engaging in 'reciprocal teaching' within cooperative groups, pupils acquire the necessary procedures to bring about changes in cognition, what Brown and Palincsar call 'learning as theory change' (p.6). Some of these procedures are mutually supportive (social) while others involve argument (conflict). For example, to facilitate group discussion, Brown and Palincsar instruct pupils to consider systematically various cases that come to mind (social) and then go on to consider counter-examples (conflict). When these social and conflict procedures are internalized and 'developed as independent cognition then learning is individualized' (p.34–9). Thus even when individuals are alone and thinking about a problem, they continue to engage in the same dialogue they would have had with other members of their group, but hold the conversation with themselves. Complex tasks which are not amenable to direct instruction are, therefore, best attempted first in mixed ability groups. Once the necessary 'scaffolding' procedures have been internalized, however, pupils can, like adults, successfully work on these tasks individually.

Facilitating Cooperative Learning

Teachers do not find it easy to manage effective cooperative group work in the primary classroom. That is why in British classrooms, as most research on the subject has shown, it is a neglected activity. Teachers argue it can be more demanding of their time than even individualization. It takes longer to set up activities; getting the group mix right is often difficult, with the result that either some children don't participate or arguments break out and lead to disruption. The teacher is therefore in and out of the groups, either repeating instructions, giving help and encouragement or resolving conflicts. With all these demands on the teacher's time it is difficult to monitor whether useful work is being done and who is doing most of it (Alexander et al., 1989).

Part of the reason for this lack of observed success is because teachers often seem to find that they need to continue direct instruction when teaching groups. However, as Galton and Williamson (1992) noted, teachers rarely first taught pupils how to work in groups so that, for example, they could resolve arguments peacefully or sum up a discussion. These scaffolding procedures are essential. Yet teacher training programmes tend to concentrate on the organizational aspects of working in groups; the pedagogic issues are rarely considered. Very few British teachers are, therefore, familiar with the procedure developed by Aronson known as jig-saw grouping or with Slavin's team games approaches. This would not be true of novice teachers in the United States where these grouping methods were developed.

Before group work can be effective, pupils have first to be instructed in how to listen to each other, how to reflect an argument and how to challenge each other without being aggressive. Teachers need to learn how to use direct instruction to teach these skills. In reciprocal teaching, for example, procedures were developed to teach pupils how to summarize, clarify and to make predictions. Pupils were invited to,

> close their eyes (metaphorically) and re-tell what they have just read as a first step towards more and more sophisticated attempts to learn how to state the gist of an argument in as few words as possible (Brown and Palincsar, 1986, p.46).

Brown argues that solving complex cognitive problems requires cooperative learning rather than direct instruction (although she doesn't call it that). When using direct instruction, an easier version of the problem is first provided and when this can be answered, error free, a more difficult version is 'faded in' (Brown and Palincsar, 1986, pp.47–9). This step then has to be repeated through incremental levels of difficulty until the learner is confronted with the mature version of the task. Since these easier versions are often pale shadows of the real task, they are often unrecognizable as facsimiles of the final task. But the more one simplifies the problem initially to make it easier and more manageable, the less it is likely to resemble the more complex end product. It is better to start with the authentic problem but to provide an appropriate supportive framework. To teach pupils how to make use of this framework, the teacher first provides a model of expert behaviour by role playing and modelling a more mature version of the activities, 'thus making them overt, explicit and concrete'. To do this successfully, the teacher must operate with a clear set of instructional goals. However, both Galton and Williamson (1992) and Bennett (1992) have observed that very often in collaborative settings, teachers, while offering explicit guidance on the task demand and the desired outcome (what to do and how to do it), rarely offer any explanation of why the collaborative strategy is being used. For example, Galton and Williamson (1992) describe a lesson where the main aim was to improve collaborative skills by jointly solving the problem of constructing a device out of various materials that would time two minutes exactly. The introduction, which lasted for nearly 20 minutes, was mainly about the importance of time. No procedures for working together on the task were elaborated, nor were the benefits of collaboration mentioned. When the children went to their groups they largely ignored the teacher's instruction to examine the materials and to spend time thinking about how they would solve the problem. Instead, they began immediately to construct a number of different models, mostly unworkable, by trial and error with very little prior discussion. The observer commented that some pupils must have questioned the usefulness of the exercise since, if accurate timing was as important as the teacher claimed, it would have surely been better to use a cheap digital watch!

Galton and Williamson (1992, pp.120–21) have summarized their own and other recommendations for facilitating collaboration in groups, as follows:

1 The value the teacher places on collaboration must be clearly communicated to the pupils. This is particularly important where collaborative groups are used for only a limited range of activities.
2 Children need first to be taught how to collaborate by breaking down activities into small steps designed to improve certain competencies and skills, such as listening, handling disagreements, etc.
3 Once these conditions have been met it is best to begin with small practical activities requiring a specific solution rather than beginning with open ended problem solving. When more abstract tasks are set, it appears useful if the task can be limited so that not too many possibilities and problems need to be taken into account. Once, however, insight has been gained into the different roles participants can play within the group and pupils have developed a sense of group identity, the quality and quantity of pupil interaction no longer tends to depend on the make up of the class nor is the size of the group so critical.
4 As the quantity of teacher feedback given to pupils about their work increases and is about the quality of their work rather than concerned with correcting mistakes (i.e. critical rather than evaluative) then the pupils will work more independently of the teacher. When evaluative teacher feedback is given it should be delivered to the class in general rather than a group in particular.
5 In collaborative work of this kind, pupils need to have confidence that teachers understand what it feels like to work in groups so that they will not, for example, be accused of time wasting when they are in fact discussing.

Much of the above research has taken place in classrooms where relationships within the classroom between pupils were, at least, tolerable. However, Cowie and her colleagues have documented the many problems which can arise in classrooms where the atmosphere can often be tense. In their study of multi-ethnic classrooms, they found certain pupils tended to dominate and use their power to 'bully' others. Not all bullying in this situation was physical. There were numerous incidents of 'bossiness', which consisted of aggressive remarks, name-calling, 'put downs' and persistent teasing. Although, as a result of working together, other pupils in the group did come to appreciate the effects of such verbal behaviour on the victims, and to deplore it, this peer pressure did not cause the incidence of bullying to decline. Cowie concluded that for teachers to cope in this situation extra resources and special training in the use of counselling skills may be necessary (Cowie *et al.*, 1994).

Social Relationships in the Classroom

This latter point – the need for a positive classroom ethos to facilitate effective collaboration – raises issues which, so far, have not been addressed, namely consideration of learning as a social as well as a cognitive activity. Research has consistently shown that pupils' willingness to activate what they already know to solve fresh problems is dependent on the strength of belief in their own capabilities. Social learning theorists such as Bandura (1986), argue that children gain in 'self-efficacy' by imitation and modelling behaviour which they find acceptable. When such modelling happens unconsciously, pupils are favourably surprised by their success and gain in confidence as a result. Much of what pupils find acceptable in the behaviour of others, particularly the teacher, will depend on the nature of the classroom relationships which are developed over time. In considering the nature of these relationships it is essential to recognize that the classroom or the school is not the same as other environments such as the home or playground. Within the classroom a very special set of power relationships operate (Warham, 1993). Observation of ways in which children behave and think within, say, the family structure may, therefore, not be replicated in the school setting.

Certainly the evidence collected from questioning pupils about how they perceive their school, for example Barrett (1986) and Galton *et al.* (1991), has shown that children, even those who just starting school, viewed classroom learning as 'work' rather than 'enlightenment' or fun. Rising 5s, for example, talked about having to 'finish our jobs'. In another instance, where pupils cooperated in building a tower consisting of large plastic hollow cubes during play-time, but were off-task during the previous lesson when it was their assigned activity, they justified this behaviour by explaining that they were 'playing' and not 'working'. When asked by the observer to explain the difference, these pupils replied, 'Work is what you do with the teacher'! In this climate, particularly with the emphasis, as it often is, on finishing our jobs 'to please the teacher', it is difficult to see how pupils can move easily from 'other' regulation to 'self' regulation of learning in the manner prescribed by Brown and Palincsar (1986). Teachers know from experience that if children are to tackle tasks independently, with a minimum of adult support, they must be confident and self-motivated to learn. How to achieve this state, however, has been a neglected feature in the study of classroom learning.

A key element concerns the links between pupils' behaviour and their self-concept. Children build up a picture about themselves which has to do with their academic and physical (games, activities, etc.) performance and with their social relationships. This is linked closely to their own personal evaluation of these self-concepts, how they value this picture of themselves. Such evaluations are generally referred to as self-esteem. Pupils build up this picture largely from the messages they receive from others, particularly their teacher and their peers. If they are uncertain of their worth, pupils may resort to the kind of behaviour which has been termed dependency. They do only what they think others want them to do so that they can avoid what they presume will be further rejection. Children who have a very low self-esteem will sometimes adopt a strategy of extreme dependency which is known as 'learned helplessness'. These pupils will claim that they 'don't know what to do', have no ideas, can't find anything, and so on. Unless they are given constant attention they give up.

Researchers such as Pollard (1985) and Galton (1989) in the United Kingdom, and Doyle (1986) in the United Stated, have all pointed to the dilemmas involved when seeking to maintain pupils' self-esteem while setting more complex, intellectually demanding tasks. Such tasks usually require learning 'as theory change' to occur, that is they demand that pupils should challenge what they already know. Pollard argues that to do this children must have a sense of ownership of their work. But it follows, since this 'picture of themselves' is based, in part, on what pupils already know, that requiring them to question their existing knowledge base carries the risk that the value they attach to this picture may decrease. The more intellectually demanding the task, the more chance there is of perceived failure and the bigger the risk to the pupils' self-esteem. Really confident pupils may not experience such problems, once they understand that the process of challenging one's ideas to construct and reconstruct what one knows is the sign of a mature thinker. For such pupils, therefore, the form of instruction or the nature of the classroom climate appears to have little effect on their capacity to learn. Presumably some of these confident pupils, because they do well academically, will eventually occupy positions of influence in adult life. Those whose influence extends to educational policy making often then tend to assume that what worked for them will work for all children.

For most pupils, however, classroom learning is more problematic. Slower learning and average pupils, and those often described as 'bright but silly' need to learn how to own up to their failures as well as their successes without it adversely affecting their perceptions of themselves. To create a supportive classroom climate which facilitates this process is not an easy task. Galton (1989) has argued that a crucial element in developing this positive climate concerns the strategies used for controlling pupil behaviour. In most classes where children are encouraged to think for themselves, the message still seems to be 'when we are concerned with learning I want you to *do as you think* but when we are concerned with behaviour I want you to *do as I say*'. Galton and Williamson (1992) showed from an analysis of pupils' responses to pictures of classroom incidents and from follow-up interviews, that children were frequently unable to make sense of this distinction, particularly in its more subtle forms. When discussing in groups, for example, pupils would be talking and the teacher would praise them for the quality of their ideas. On another occasion, when they were still 'on-task' but 'were not getting anywhere', they would be 'told off' for chatting and wasting time. When these pupils were presented with pictures of a group of children working on mathematical calculations, and asked what the teacher was saying, the overwhelming number of suggested comments were disciplinary and negative. The children in the pictures were being told to 'do it again' or exhorted to 'get on with it'. They were asked, 'Can't you get anything right?' The frequency of these kind of comments increased if pupils were initially told, 'The girl (boy) in the picture has got her (his) sum wrong. What is the teacher saying?' These pupil perceptions hardy accord with the view expressed by one of the 'Three Wise Men' (p.93) that primary teachers were reluctant to criticize their pupils!

Pupils, therefore, appear to see classroom activity as a single entity and do not make the distinctions that teachers would like them to make. Pupils resent being 'told off' for chatting because they have not completed the group task when, from their perspective, they had overrun the time allowed for discussion because of interest in the topic. When teachers ask questions pupils are unsure whether it is to find out what they know or whether they are paying attention. This kind of ambiguity of task, to which Doyle (1986) refers, tends to create dependency. Pupils wait for a class-mate to interact with the teacher so they can get clues about what is expected in a given context.

It is important, given the anti-progressive rhetoric of most education policy makers, that any attempt to remove such ambiguities should not imply that teachers condone bad behaviour nor that it should remain unchecked. In any case, no teacher wishes to preside over a classroom which has degenerated into anarchy. But while not condoning bad behaviour, teachers should convey to their pupils the message that they understand the reasons why this behaviour took place (Deci and Ryan, 1985). Galton and Williamson (1992) quote an example of a teacher who made use of this principle. In her classroom, a boy hit a girl and made her cry. This girl was being teased about 'fancying' one of the boy pupils. She had lashed out catching the boy on the shoulder and he had retaliated more forcibly. The teacher was very quick to reprimand both pupils for the disturbance, particularly the boy. As often happens when events of this kind take place, the atmosphere in the classroom changed. Whereas before it had been relaxed and friendly it was now tense and the pupils continued working in silence. At this point the teacher looked up and said casually, to no one in particular, 'This boy and girl thing is very funny, isn't it?'. She then went on to tell the class about an incident that happened to her when she was their age and went with her mother to visit her aunt. There was also a cousin present, a boy of roughly her own age. After tea she and the cousin were told that they could go and play in the boy's bedroom. As they went to leave the room her aunt said to them, 'Don't you get up to any funny business when the two of you go to the bedroom'! At this point in the story the teacher paused for a moment and then said quietly to the class, who were all paying rapt attention, 'I wasn't half embarrassed! My face went all red.' By now the tenseness had dissolved and when the class returned to their work the atmosphere was relaxed and friendly once more.

Here we have an excellent example of what Deci and Ryan called 'honest evaluations', where the teacher, while not condoning anti-social actions, tries to convey to the class that she understands these often occur as a result of human weakness rather than because of serious character defects. In so doing, the teacher indicates to the offending children that they are 'not beyond the pale' so that good relationships can continue. In the above account the atmosphere immediately relaxed after the story because the children, while accepting the reprimand, understood they had not seriously damaged their relationship with the teacher.

Within this form of relationship it becomes possible to negotiate rules for behaviour as well as learning so that, as far as possible, ambiguity is eliminated. This does not mean teachers giving into pupils. But it does mean that teachers must be prepared to articulate their needs so that pupils can take these into account when deciding on a course of action while learning how to 'regulate' their own behaviour. Often, however, teachers are reluctant to 'own up' to their problems in case they lose the respect of the children. For example, rather than admit to their concerns in a situation where too many pupils are talking loudly, a teacher may accuse the class of 'being too noisy'. In such situations, Deci and Chandler (1986, p.591) argue that rather than trying to 'con' the pupils into believing that they are doing things such as tidying up, not for the teacher's sake but for their own good, it is better to 'come clean' and admit, 'I feel better when the classroom is neat and tidy'. This approach is just as appropriate when there is excessive noise, since there are valid reasons why this is unacceptable to the teacher (e.g., it is difficult to hear what other pupils are saying).

Galton quotes another example of a teacher who wasted ten minutes every day rounding up the children from the playground. Discussion of the problem led both sides to state their needs: from the teacher's point of view he was worried the head would react unfavourably because he seemed to have an undisciplined class, and from the pupils' point of view, they hated walking in a crocodile and being marched in to the classroom. Together the class and the teacher negotiated a solution which was acceptable to both sides, namely for the teacher to walk from the staff-room when the bell rang and for the pupils to walk to the class-room from the playground. The system worked beautifully but as the teacher said in his conclusion,

> We saved ten minutes a day in the round ups and in the time that I used to spend lecturing them on lining up and marching quietly. But the biggest difference is about how we feel about each other when we get into the room. Everybody used to be mad by the time we had lined up and now we go into the room feeling good and that sometimes saves a whole afternoon. (Galton, 1989, pp.161–2)

In most cases, although relationships are, on the surface, warm and friendly, ambiguity remains because not understanding the teacher's needs, pupils cannot always understand the reasons for the teacher's decisions. In practice, this makes it difficult to encourage children to use the strategies involved in reciprocal teaching and cooperative learning. For example, with the most-used form of classroom control – 'Don't smile until Christmas' – pupils are always uncertain when the teacher will revert to a 'firm' regime in place of the relaxed friendly atmosphere. Rogers (1990) provides many helpful hints for teachers who wish to move away from this approach and to create positive climates which build up the pupil's self-esteem. This includes a chapter on conflict resolution and the importance of avoiding, in all but the most extreme cases, using what Galton (1989) has described as 'dog training' procedures. These involve teachers using key phrases such as 'listen' and routines such as 'Simon says' to bring the class under control. These techniques are not dissimilar to those key commands used to train dogs. 'Listen', 'hands on heads', 'fingers on lips' are very reminiscent of commands such as 'sit' or 'heel'! Rogers, with long experience of teaching, accepts that these strategies are sometimes required in extreme cases but gives advice on how such situations can be retrieved and positive relationships re-established. He concludes:

> Today, personal dynamics in the classroom are subject to high emotion and fallibility but that only increases the need to plan for the sorts of things you ought to say and do when we discipline. It is possible to develop personal school-wide discipline that is more decisive and less reactive without losing that fundamental humanity. That not only makes teaching bearable but even enjoyable. Rogers, 1990, p.276)

This, of course, leads on to a key question, namely why is it, despite the accounts of the very stressful experiences that many teachers have when managing today's primary classrooms, there is a marked reluctance to engineer shifts in pedagogy along these lines. This is particularly true of the inner-city schools where the power structures which teachers attempt to maintain in the classroom are no longer accepted by pupils who, in many cases, have learned to confront more extreme examples of adult dominance on the streets (Warham, 1993). It is interesting, for example, that in Cowie *et al.'s* (1994) account of attempts to develop cooperative learning in multi-ethnic inner-city schools, although the teachers attempted to get children to use 'tit for tat' negotiating skills for dealing with aggression in groups, there are no accounts of teachers rethinking their own behaviour management strategy. However, it is one thing to establish a set of pedagogic principles but another to promote them effectively during both initial training and INSET. This matter will be discussed further in the final chapter but before beginning this discussion the main pedagogic principles to emerge from this chapter will be summarized.

Chapter 6
Raising Standards: Developing Expertise in Teaching

Before attempting to tackle the question of changing current classroom practice in the primary school, it is perhaps necessary to bring together the ideas from the previous chapter. It was argued that, in so far as teachers have received any advice on improving their teaching, the ideas put forward have essentially been concerned with classroom organization, planning and assessment. These are all, in the main, to do with strategic questions and have little to say about teaching at a tactical level, which is the main concern of pedagogy. Although the nature of the learning will have some bearing on strategic decisions, they will be strongly influenced by contextual variables. For example, classroom organization is primarily determined by a combination of the task demand, the composition of the class and the immediate environment where the teaching takes place. A school's approach to planning the curriculum will depend, to a great extent, on the degree of staff competence in different subject areas. In other words, such decisions are primarily managerial ones.

Tactics, on the other hand, are concerned with classroom transactions, that is, the exchanges between teachers and pupils and between pupils and pupils. Although tactics are related to strategy they are not driven by it, as is assumed in much of the advice emanating from HMI and the late National Curriculum Council. For example, under present classroom conditions it appears easier to facilitate exchanges involving what are termed 'higher order questions' in whole-class settings. But if we could change the strategic conditions, as did the teachers in the ORACLE study who were called 'infrequent changers', then similar high levels of questioning can take place during one-to-one interactions.

Researchers interested in these tactical issues do not dispute that the management functions of teaching, as displayed in the work of the 'teacher effectiveness movement', lead to an improvement in learning outcomes, particularly those measured by standardized tests. They do believe, however, that, ultimately, standards will only rise when the study of pedagogy, the use of appropriate teaching tactics to facilitate the learning processes involved in any task demand, becomes a central element of a teacher's professional development. This requires the teacher to know something about teaching and about learning processes and the relationship between the two. That is why pedagogy has been defined as the 'science of the art of teaching'.

Most official advice to teachers on practice ignores this view of pedagogy, implying that teachers can work out these links between teaching and learning by 'trial and error'. For example, in the 'Three Wise Men's' report the main issues are to do with classroom organization and assessment. Although the report does argue that teaching methods should be chosen using the criterion of 'fitness for purpose', and that this should include some analysis of the 'goals of learning', these goals appear to refer to the task demands rather that the cognitive processes involved. The report does make some attempt to introduce a theoretical perspective on learning, based on an alternative to Piaget's model of child development but this is not carried through in any detail. Instead, the 'Three Wise Men' criticize the over-reliance on theory (by implication Piaget's) in the development of contemporary practice. Throughout this book it has been argued that this view is wrong and that, for the most part, primary practice is pragmatically driven at a strategic rather than a tactical level. The current problems have largely arisen because in this situation strategy then determines tactics instead of the other way round. However, the 'Three Wise Men' had almost nothing to say on this issue and consequently failed to indicate clearly how teachers might make appropriate choices of different teaching methods according to 'fitness for purpose'. Rather than blame the weaknesses of primary practice upon 'theory', a strong case can be made for saying that the fault lies with those in senior positions within the 'educational establishment' who have failed to engage with these issues intellectually and, as a result, have been unable to offer much in the way of useful advice on the subject.

Chapter 5, therefore, attempted to add that extra dimension to the discussion by exploring the pedagogic issues embedded in such statements as 'fitness for purpose'. It began by rejecting the notion that an effective pedagogy can be created solely by the application of the teacher's 'common sense appraisal' of what is and what is not effective. This is because a teacher's perception of what goes on in the classroom is selective and generally attributes causality to factors which lie outside their personal control. Thus, failures of pupils to learn are not blamed on the way the topic was taught but to external factors to do with the children's home background or their limited powers of concentration.

Interestingly, as Cortazzi (1991) has demonstrated, teachers also rarely claim credit for any outstanding pupil achievement. Because, therefore, the teachers' analysis of classroom problems places less emphasis on possible weaknesses in their own behaviour, the teaching solutions chosen will tend to suit the teacher but may not be best suited to the pupils' needs. What is required, therefore, are other sources of ideas about teaching and learning that can be used to validate the teacher's own analysis. Among such sources would be theories of how children learn to think.

This then raised the issue of how, given that there exists no clear-cut view about children's development, it is possible for teachers to use theory in conjunction with their own common sense experience to select the most appropriate teaching methods. It was suggested that the third element in this verification procedure could be the empirical data collected from process-product classroom observation studies. The evidence from these studies suggests that the use of direct instruction (not to be confused with direct teaching) is most appropriate for teaching pupils to solve relatively simple problems involving procedural routines, content knowledge and factual information. The teacher's role in this kind of problem-solving is very similar to the computer programmer who provides the machine with the procedures necessary to work out a solution. As well as the actual calculation, this also involves routines for accessing, storing and retrieving information and rules for making decisions (e.g., how to proceed if a result is higher or lower than a given value). Decision making in a computer consists of answering lots of these 'yes or no' questions very quickly. The efficiency of the computer depends on this speed of processing and its capacity to store large amounts of information in chunks. The effectiveness is also increased by the use of 'sub-routines'. These are regularly used procedures which can be automatically called up when needed rather than starting from scratch each time.

When this information model of 'man as a computer' is applied to learning by direct instruction there are strong parallels. The pupils are given new information, they are shown how to remember it and are taught how to use it in various procedures to solve problems. The pupils then practise these procedures until they can use them automatically. However, just as with the simple computer model, where if the nature of the problem-solving changes appreciably the computer has to be reprogrammed, so too when we move from teaching how to multiply whole numbers to multiplying fractions or decimals, we have to begin the process of direct instruction again. Once we move to generalities, for example understanding the principles of multiplication irrespective of the particular application, direct instruction appears to be less effective. This form of thinking or concept development involves the acquisition of new ideas (or the invention of them) and an ability to make appropriate use of them. In the process we may have to identify the nature of a problem, analyse its components, determine whether we have sufficient knowledge to solve it and be able to monitor whether our efforts are likely to be productive. This ability to regulate our thinking processes, or to 'control the domain of cognition' (Meadows, 1993, p.78) lies at the heart of what in Chapter 5 was called 'learning as theory change'. The 'man as a computer' model isn't very helpful for understanding these 'metacognitive' processes but the ideas of Vygotsky, based upon cooperative learning, are. Here the more competent help the less competent move to a position where they can become 'self-regulating' in their thinking. To assist the less competent learner, the more competent must provide a 'scaffolding' or framework by means of which these metacognitive processes can be internalized. Once this state is achieved the pupil can become an independent thinker. They still need to engage in the same metacognitive processes but now 'talk to themselves' rather than with peers or an adult. The teacher's role is now primarily that of facilitator and 'friendly critic', as described in the Piagetian account of the thinking process. Thus Vygotsky and Piaget represent the ends of a continuum which moves from 'other' to 'self' regulation.

For example, part of the scaffolding for discussion during collaborative learning involves systematically considering all cases in support of the argument, then all counter examples. Cases which are neither for nor against are then isolated and used to suggest possible alternative ways of presenting the original proposition (Brown and Palincsar, 1986, p.39). Groups are taught to apply this strategy until the process becomes automatic. These procedures, therefore, along with more fundamental skills such as learning to listen carefully, communicate one's views and handle conflict within the group, need to be taught initially through direct instruction. Whether the teacher or peer provides the scaffolding depends on contextual factors. Brown and Palincsar (1986) argue that the more abstract the problem the more dominant will be the teacher's participation. Much will depend on the extent to which the more competent pupils within the class have internalized the scaffolding procedures.

Decisions about classroom organization should then follow from this analysis. In direct instruction, class teaching will be most effective because it maximizes teacher contact. Thus when teaching procedures or skills such as listening, the whole class can be involved. When new information is being offered, including demonstrations of relatively simple problem-solving using this information, ability groups are likely to be preferred. Once, however, thinking processes involve metacognition (getting ideas for story writing, hypothesis generation, evaluating historical evidence, etc.) mixed ability groups are required. This suggests that the current practice of having two different subject areas in operation, but with one requiring direct instruction and the other cooperative learning in groups, should be the preferred strategy.

However, even with this strategy in place there remains a question of motivating pupils to participate enthusiastically in these activities. Studies show that even when pupils have the necessary prior knowledge they appear reluctant to engage in more demanding cognitive activities, preferring instead to feign dependency. This aspect of learning was totally neglected in the advice emanating from the National Curriculum Council, OFSTED and the 'Three Wise Men'. In studies such as Brown and Palincsar's, the ratio of adults to pupils was relatively high. Thus pupils could continue to operate within a 'dependency mode'. Once the researchers have departed, however, this would not be a feasible strategy. Research suggests that it is only possible to use this approach in classes with one adult if the pupils' self-image and self-esteem (both academic and social) are high. If pupils feel confident enough in their learning so that they do not fear failure, they will be more willing to initiate exchanges with teachers in which they are open about the difficulties they have encountered and the solutions they have used in attempting to solve a problem.

In Chapter 5 it was argued that much of the current dependency is created by the discontinuity which exists between the management of learning and the management of behaviour in the primary classroom. Learning is managed so that pupils are expected to do as they think, while in matters of behaviour teachers require pupils to do as they say. This invests more complex learning tasks with a degree of ambiguity in that pupils are never certain of what teachers require of them in a particular situation, whether the teacher's utterance is concerned primarily with learning or with control. Consequently the pupils 'hedge their bets' and use various avoidance strategies to ensure the teacher initially interacts with another member of the class. By watching and listening carefully to this initial exchange, the rest of the class are able to discern the teacher's intentions.

More than any other part of their practice, teachers, once they have acquired an effective means of classroom control, tend to stick with it for the remainder of their teaching lives. The approach they favour will largely depend on their experience during initial training and the practice favoured by their mentors. There is, therefore, a case for things remaining as they are and leaving teachers to continue to do what they already do while helping them become more effective classroom lecturers and disciplinarians. However, research suggests that such an approach will not create a classroom climate which encourages creativity and persuades pupils of the value of solving difficult problems cooperatively. These are skills which industrialists tell us will be required of workers in the twenty-first century. It would seem, therefore, despite the calls of government ministers and of the media for a return to more traditional teaching approaches, that there is little option but to continue the search for ways of successfully implementing these necessary changes in pedagogy.

Why is it so Difficult to Change Classroom Practice?

When looking for effective ways of changing classroom practice, one is confronted with a 'chicken and egg' situation. Is it best to reform the way we teach teachers to teach or should we concentrate on changing the practice of experienced teachers? This dilemma arises because it is clear, not only from research evidence (Kagan, 1992) but also from talking to students teachers, that the main formative influences during initial training occur in the period the students spend in school on continuous practice. When searching for a 'survival strategy' during their initial encounters in the classroom, new teachers will naturally model themselves upon their more experienced supervising teacher. Even if true, as alleged by certain critics, that the training institutions provide students with a 'heavy diet' of progressive theory, it is doubtful whether this influences how these novice teachers approach the task of facing a class for the first time.

Given the powerful influence of modelling on practice, there is a great deal to be said for allowing new teachers to have a very heavy immersion in schools, initially, before bringing them out of the classroom and challenging the assumptions about learning on which these newly acquired forms of practice appear to be based. This is certainly the thinking behind David Hargreaves' (1990) suggestion of creating training schools along the same lines as teaching hospitals. Hargreaves' views have been attacked, particularly because he also argues that the financial management of teacher training should reside with the schools. Those working in the present university education departments would only be called upon if schools felt they had something valuable to offer. At its best, this approach could solve the 'chicken and egg' dilemma by creating more interest in pedagogy among teachers. Staff with the main responsibility for inducting new recruits into the profession would also have an INSET role and be required to articulate their own ideas about teaching and learning more clearly. In this task they would need the help of classroom researchers and even, perhaps, developmental psychologists!

However, given that the 'New Right' have also advocated ending the involvement of university education departments in training, not to stimulate an interest in pedagogy but to end what they 'see as their unnecessary and subversive role in the preparation of new teachers' (Edwards, 1994), a constructive debate about the value of Hargreaves' ideas has not been possible. Instead, he has been regarded by many as betraying the interests of his own professional group. However, Lawlor's (1990) proposals and similar offerings from the 'New Right' (Hillgate Group, 1989; O'Hear, 1988) would do nothing to end the ineffectiveness of existing models whereby new teachers learn to teach like old teachers and considerable sums are then spent attempting to persuade old teachers to adopt new practices. The net result of such an approach is always to have another group of older teachers who need retraining!

Those colleagues who fail to understand the reasoning behind Hargreaves' suggestion of a totally school-based approach at the initial stage would also probably reject the above analysis of what happened under the college-based system of training. These tutors dislike using the words 'teacher training' to describe their courses, preferring the term, 'teacher education'. While conceding that students are heavily influenced by their initial encounters with teachers in schools they, nevertheless, argue that the educational principles learned during this time resurface at a later date, once teachers have settled into the profession and the somewhat artificial situation of pretending to be a 'proper' teacher in someone else's class has been satisfactorily negotiated. Unfortunately, there is little research evidence to attest that a delayed reaction to training of this sort does occur. During the last decade, therefore, in an attempt to counter the criticisms about the irrelevance of theory, most institutions have adopted some version of the 'partnership' model.

The first approaches of this kind were developed in the early 1980s at the University of Sussex and at Leicester (Everton and Impey, 1989). Later, a different model with the emphasis on mentoring rather than co-tutoring was developed at the University of Oxford, Department of Education (Benton, 1990). The original Sussex model, where students spent the greater part of the course in schools, coming into the university for tutorials in which they attempted to make sense of these diverse experiences, enjoyed certain practical advantages over more traditional courses. First, students were happier when they were in schools and second, it was a lot cheaper (at the time schools made only a small charge for offering this service). The Leicester model was more theoretically-based and used the IT-INSET approach developed by Ashton *et al.* (1989). Unlike the Sussex programme, IT-INSET was very expensive because it demanded that the university tutor should be in the school alongside the teacher-tutor and the student so that theory-practice dilemmas could be discussed during post-lesson tutorials. In this approach, the classroom was viewed as an experimental laboratory with all participants working to make sense of events. Unlike the conventional apprenticeship model, where the supervising teacher might say to a student who wanted to try something new, 'I tried this and it didn't work', Ashton's approach was to encourage teachers to respond by saying, 'It didn't work for me. Let's see together if we can find out why'.

Evaluation of these school-based approaches by Furlong *et al.* (1988) showed, however, that they were not totally successful for a number of reasons. First – and this applied to the IT-INSET approach in particular – the partnership was not democratic, in the sense that the teacher, student and university tutor had equal status in the decision making. The power relationships were such that often the tutor's views dominated the post-lesson tutorials. This led to the second weakness, that the tutor's views were not, as the theory envisaged, informed by any deep knowledge of pedagogy for all the reasons set out by Simon (1981b). Opinions expressed during tutorials were, therefore, largely atheorectical in contrast to the 'New Right's' charge that current practice is distorted by 'the subversive influences of alien theory' emanating from the universities. Anyone who doubts the truth of this statement has only to inspect feedback comments that university tutors record in their students' teaching practice files.

Nevertheless, the notion of 'partnership' between the schools and the university department of education has now become the accepted orthodoxy (Edwards, 1994). Students are encouraged to 'reflect critically on their practice' in order to change it for the better. The interpretation of the term, 'the reflective practitioner' has not always been clear (Calderhead, 1987). In particular, as McIntyre (1992) argues, there remains much confusion about the relationship between this activity called 'reflection' and 'the process of theorising'. According to McIntyre, the most common usage of the term 'reflection' in teacher education appears to be of the kind proposed by Lucas (1991). This mainly involves 'systematic enquiry into one's own practice to improve that practice and deepen one's understanding of it'. This view accords with the idea of developing 'craft' theories of pedagogy in the manner suggested by Schon (1983) and was the central idea behind IT-INSET.

Novice Teachers as Reflective Practioners

The extensive research on differences between novice and expert teachers (Berliner, 1992) raises serious doubts whether students on initial teaching courses are able to reflect on their practice in this way. Unlike expert teachers, novices are unable quickly to identify meaningful classroom patterns but tend to concentrate on discrete events (Carter *et al.*, 1988). There are particular problems for new students when they attempt to make sense of apparently conflicting sources of data. For example, some of the class may be working enthusiastically, some may be 'off task' while the majority are in that 'in-between stage' where, unless swift action is taken, the general level of motivation will rapidly decline. Understandably, novices are not very sensitive to such situations. Consequently, since their representation of the problem is qualitatively different from the expert teacher, they lack an overall strategy to deal with the situation. Lacking this 'holistic' view they, instead, attempt to deal with each aspect of the problem in turn, therefore making it more likely that a breakdown will occur in one area of the classroom while they are dealing with another problem elsewhere.

Another important difference between the expert and the novice is the former's ability to take into account seemingly unconnected contextual factors in planning and carrying out a classroom activity. Thus, rain (indoor playtime), or a report by a dinner lady of a disturbance during lunch, may cause the expert teacher to restructure a practical lesson or abandon it altogether in favour of a more formal activity involving seat work. Expert teachers, unlike the novice, are therefore, in Borko and Livingston's (1989) terms, 'improvisational performers'. This quality of flexibility derives from the way they engage in problem-solving. Experts are very proficient at using a repertoire of routines which Galton (1989) refers to as 'exiting' strategies. Over the years experts develop routines for dealing with certain patterns of classroom events but they also realize that the context in which these patterns occur is rarely likely to be the same from one occasion to the other. Thus, however carefully planned the lesson, it is unlikely to be completed within the time allowed. Experts can judge quite early on in the lesson where they are likely to be by the end, and can make it appear that the point at which they finish is nevertheless the natural point for a break. A novice, however, concentrates on 'entry' strategies designed to eliminate the interruptions which caused the planning to breakdown in the first place. On some training courses, for example, novices are taught to put approximate times against various activities when planning a lesson. Invariably, they run over time, conclude there were too many activities and make a revised plan with less content. In the next lesson, because of circumstances outside their immediate control, they again fail to finish on cue! This goes on until the experience leads the novice to the conclusion that it is unproductive to continue to plan in such an inflexible way. The use of exit rather than entry strategies is particularly relevant to the management of classroom breakdowns. Experts know that these are unpredictable and that sometimes initially low-key disruptions can lead to major confrontations if not dealt with swiftly and calmly. Most novices do not have a sense of an impending crisis until it is too late.

Lacking this holistic view of classroom events, as Berliner (1992) points out, novices are unable to make sense of patterns which would make it possible to theorize usefully about their practice in the way that Schon and others suggest. Novices usually also find it difficult to make sense of other people's theories, which is another reason why so many courses are 'atheoretical'. This is because, as Benner (1984, p.21) concludes from her study of nurse training, such rules 'legislate' against successful performance because they (the trainers) cannot tell them (the novices) the most relevant task to perform in the actual situation. Novices then come to regard this advice as 'too theoretical' while still believing that there should exist somewhere a set of guidelines or even tips which will enable them to survive as teachers, no matter what the context of their teaching. Thus the trainer may advise a student not to commence speaking at the start of a lesson until 'the class begin to settle' but the novice is unable to recognize that critical moment which determines whether the class will listen attentively or go on talking. The lesson then begins badly with the student loudly demanding silence, the advice is deemed to be worthless and blame for this is attributed to the tutor's lack of 'recent and relevant' experience!

McIntyre (1992), when writing about the Oxford parternship scheme, makes a similar point but notes that in the United States there is much more willingness on the part of trainers and students to use the findings from classroom research as a basis for reflecting on the kinds of problems which can arise when, for example, starting off a lesson. McIntrye goes on to make the same point as in the previous chapter, that this theoretical evidence does not have to be universally acknowledged as true in order to be useful. Its purpose is to provide a framework on which students can hang their reflections. In this way they may not only come to understand better some of the contextual features of classrooms but also begin to master the professional skills needed as they attempt to move beyond the novice stage. For example, Budd Rowe's (1974) classic study suggests that teachers should give pupils, particularly slow learning ones, extended time to answer questions. Reviews of research show that few teachers provide this 'wait time' (Tobin, 1983). Budd Rowe recommended that teachers should pause after asking a question (first wait-time) and then pause again after the student has given an initial response (second wait-time).

On the other hand there is a substantial body of research of long standing (e.g., Kounin, 1970) on classroom management, that advises teachers to maintain a lively pace during the lesson. In the direct instruction approach there are standard routines for questioning pupils, including rules for 'turn taking' and instructions to conduct the question and answer exchanges at a 'brisk pace' (Rosenshine, 1987). Confronted with this apparently contradictory advice, students could go into schools, observe different teachers asking questions and talk with them afterwards about reasons behind their choice of technique. Later, with the help of the university tutor, students may begin to see that in the context of direct instruction, where pupils are competing with each other to provide a right answer, attempting to put Budd Rowe's ideas into practice may cause difficulties. Extended wait-times may be more appropriate in a situation where pupils have been told that the thinking required to answer the question needs a cooperative effort. By introducing Doyle's (1986) notion of task ambiguity, and the risks involved in answering questions, the novice is offered further ideas about the use of 'turn taking' during direct instruction as a way of reducing dependency effects. The value of the jig-saw approach for minimizing risk to a pupil's self-esteem during the initial stages of group work might then be explored at a later date.

In his attempt to distinguish between different types of reflection, McIntyre (1992) argues that novices begin by reflecting at a *technical* level, in which they develop a 'a repertoire of skills' and make 'deliberate use of ideas from a wide variety of sources and also on theorising about these ideas in relation to a wide range of criteria, including some at the practical and critical levels' (p.45). The ideas concern those issues which are a priority for novice teachers to do with maintaining classroom control, gaining pupils' attention and interest and ensuring pupils understand the content of the lessons. In one sense this starting point is an obvious one, since if the student teacher cannot survive in the classroom they will be unable to go on to the next stage, which McIntyre defines as *practical* reflectivity, 'where the emphasis is on articulating one's own criteria and evaluating and developing one's own practice'.

This phase is an important one in which the students acquire the habits and skills of reflectivity and the theorizing. Reflection of this kind, as noted by Grossman (1992), usually sees novice teachers engage in deliberations about the nature of the subject that they are teaching, its principles and its methods of enquiry. Both McIntyre and Grossman base their analyses on specialist secondary teachers. It is perhaps not so easy to extend this idea to generalist primary teachers, although the emphasis on subject content within the National Curriculum may be changing things.

The third level involves the application of *critical* or *emancipatory* reflectivity. Students are required to consider the ways in which the context of schooling and of society influences events in classrooms. In the Oxford programme, novice teachers do not reflect on their own practice but investigate any disparity, both within and between the different school contexts, in which the students are placed. A similar approach is used on the Leicester professional studies course where, for example, during partnership visits, students collect information about different schools' guidelines on race or special needs and, on returning to the university, contrast these practices with 'theory' in an attempt to explain discrepancies between policy and practice. At no stage are any of these students involved in 'action research' programmes involving 'critical reflection' on their own practice. McIntyre concludes,

> Finally, in relation to process I would re-emphasise the limited role of reflection in initial teacher education. Even in relation to the three levels of reflectivity discussed here it seems clear that reflection, although important as an element in learning, is important either as a subsidiary element to the other kinds of learning and theorising or as a goal to be attained, a kind of learning to be practised and developed for future use. In addition, however, we should surely expect much more theorising to be done during initial teacher education which is not concerned with the student teacher's reflection on their individual practices. There is much to be read, to be discussed to be found in the practices of experienced teachers which merits examination and mental trial but which will not be possible for an individual student teacher to test in his or her own practice because of the constraints of time, opportunity or expertise. Reflection concerns one's present practices, but theorising concerns the whole world of possibilities for the future. (McIntyre, 1992, p.47)

Within this partnership, the research role of the tutors in the university is to concern themselves with theory which has relevance to practice. They can codify 'craft knowledge', as Galton and Williamson (1992) attempted in partnership with a teacher who was recognized as an expert in collaborative group work. Other kinds of theorizing employ the forms of conceptual analysis derived from the educational disciplines, to illuminate topics which cause concern to teachers, such as differentiation and progression. Another task is in helping teachers improve the levels of professional discourse when dealing with matters which are known to be critical to pupils' progress. This would help reduce the gap between 'rhetoric' and practice observed by Alexander (1991) in the Leeds PNP evaluation. If these activities could take place in a number of pedagogic centres closely linked with Hargreaves' 'hospital schools' offering a wide range of training, then these centres of excellence could support other kinds of partnership schemes, such as those currently operating in training institutions without a sizeable research base. Such schemes would begin to overcome Simon's (1981b) lament for the lack of a truly pedagogic base on which to construct the professional development of teachers.

Such a model, however, would be vastly different from the present government's scheme. To begin with, it requires much higher staffing levels in schools than those the government is currently able or willing to provide. Without additional resources, the present programmes of school-based work initiated by the government must, inevitably, lead to a decline in standards. Whatever the weakness of the former university-based programmes, they were relatively cheap in that many sessions were conducted in medium or large groups. This was particularly true of the professional studies courses. Under the present system, one teacher is responsible for doing much the same thing with three students as was previously undertaken with groups of 50. Even the transfer of sums of the order of £1,000 to schools barely pays for one hour a week's reflection of the kind recommended by McIntyre (1992). While, in the long term, it may be possible to attain greater efficiency by clustering schools together, the present system must, because of the widely observed diversity in practice, lead to situations in which how a student learns to teach will depend even more on the mentor with whom that student is placed. The sums which were provided for training during the transition have barely been able to 'scratch the surface' of this problem. In most cases the money has only been sufficient to enable mentors to have an average of four days training. Meanwhile, university tutors are visiting schools for informal consultations less frequently because they must now earn the money paid out in support of school-based training.

There is also a clear conflict of interest under the present system between the role of mentor and the role of classroom teacher. Even when the cost of taking an experienced teacher out of the classroom is fully met, there still remains the question of whether their time is best spent with three student teachers or 30 pupils! Finally, there are questions over the division of responsibilities within the partnership. Who is to be mainly responsible for teaching the application of subject knowledge and who for pedagogy? Are these two aspects of practice distinguishable and, if so, where should the balance lie? These issues have taken on more significance as a result of the 'Three Wise Men's' call for more specialist subject teaching in the top half of the junior school. However, the case for adopting this course may not be so convincing as it appears at first sight.

How Much Subject Knowledge do Primary Teachers Need?

Currently, a considerable amount of the government's INSET budget is being devoted to increasing the subject knowledge of primary teachers so that they can deliver the National Curriculum programmes of study more effectively. The policy agenda, besides the argument for increased specialization, includes provision of intensive training packages for subject coordinators and proposals for a broad-based shortened B.Ed. degree in the core and foundation subjects. To limit the amount of knowledge required, and therefore costs, the demands of the National Curriculum at Key Stages 1 and 2 are being reduced.

In the previous chapter, practice, as defined by HMI and senior officials of the National Curriculum Council, was shown to be mainly concerned with strategic decisions to do with planning, organizational management and assessment. There is a clear assumption that all these aspects will improve when teachers know more about their subject, first, because they will gain the necessary confidence to risk modifying their existing practice and second, because different subjects are distinguished by 'different ways of knowing'. These ways have to do not only with the subject matter but also its structure, the nature of the evidence used to support a proposition and the methods typically used to solve problems. This kind of knowledge, categorized mainly under the headings in Table 5.1 as discipline and strategic knowledge, should enable teachers to anticipate likely difficulties pupils face when engaged on a particular task or when attempting to solve a particular problem. As a result of increasing their subject knowledge, teachers should plan their lessons more coherently and assess them more appropriately. During the lesson, teachers should be able to offer better explanations, chose more appropriate examples and make feasible inferences concerning the difficulties pupils experience. Studies of primary teachers by Bennett and Carré (1993) and Summers (1994) have both shown that there are large gaps in primary teachers' knowledge of this kind in English, mathematics and, in particular, science.

However, in the previous chapter a different view of practice 'as pedagogy' was put forward. This had more to do with general principles of learning and with ways of motivating children to learn. It placed less emphasis on planning and preparation, monitoring and assessment and more on pupil-teacher and pupil-pupil relationships. Clearly teachers must have some knowledge of their subject, but are improvements in their existing knowledge base a sufficient guarantee that practice will improve and that children will learn more as a result? These questions have been taken up by, among others, Lee Shulman (1986, 1987) and Pamela Grossman (1992).

Shulman's original concern was with the claims made by those conducting process-product research, particularly the claims resulting from research on direct instruction. At one stage there was a tendency to claim that improved management of such matters as time on task, and the mastery of routine procedures such as questioning, were the sole determinants of increased pupil progress. Shulman was reacting against this proposition, although he was careful to point out in a footnote that he did not wish to deny the importance of what he termed 'pedagogical knowledge of teaching'; he *did* wish to argue that what also mattered was the quality of instruction and that this was not simply a question of subject matter. Subject knowledge involved, as explained earlier, the way subject matter was organized (its structure) and also the rules which enabled any proposition to be determined as true or false. According to Shulman, a teacher not only had to know that 'something was so' but also 'why it was so'. This leads on to the argument that teachers' knowledge of the 'structures' of their subject informs a pedagogy to do with understanding what makes certain topics difficult to learn, which explanations best represent ideas and which strategies are most useful in reorganizing the understanding of learners. This Shulman called 'pedagogical content knowledge' to distinguish it from 'pedagogical knowledge of teaching'. However, it should be clear from the previous chapter that there is a degree of overlap in the two constructs, particularly as they relate to the development of 'scaffolding' to 'reorganize the understanding of learners'. In Shulman's case this pedagogic knowledge is primarily determined by the knowledge of the subject, while in Chapter 5 it was based on an understanding of the processes involved in 'learning to think'.

Returning to the question of the need for greater subject expertise among primary teachers, there has been a tendency to polarize the debate about the importance that should be given to the different types of pedagogy. As a result, questions dealing with the way that subject knowledge interacts with knowledge about teaching have been neglected. This includes the question raised in the previous chapter as to why pupils who appear to have all the necessary conceptual knowledge do not activate it when asked to use it for tasks in school. The debate about pedagogy in relation to the National Curriculum has been driven by this limited view of pedagogy to do with planning and preparation, managing of input and monitoring. Considerable resources have been put into increasing the knowledge base of primary teachers but so far the evidence from the surveys of current practice at Key Stages 1 and 2, as reported in Chapters 2 and 3, has not indicated marked improvements in these aspects of practice, other than in planning.

Perhaps two further doubts can be expressed about this approach. First, is the existing knowledge base sufficiently strong to build on, particularly in science? It is a well-established fact that, in terms of prior qualifications, entrants into B.Ed. courses tend to have the lowest A-level grades. Accepting that such grades are not everything (before two A-levels were compulsory, Nottingham University's B.Ed classification correlated more highly with O-level grades!) they do reflect the amount of academic knowledge of a subject, as opposed, possibly, to a candidate's general intellectual capabilities. Given the shortage of recruits with qualifications in mathematics and science, where the grades are weakest, converting students with arts backgrounds into scientific experts is always going to be costly and difficult. Indeed, Summers (1994) reports on 'slippage' in what even primary teachers with science backgrounds were able to learn during in-service training. Summers reports similar experiences in the United States and describes the teachers' grasp of the concepts of force and energy as 'messy'. He concludes that the existing improvement can only be sustained by means of regular 'bursts' of further INSET, both in the laboratory and in the classroom.

The second source of doubt comes from studies of the way teachers who have expert knowledge use it in the classroom. Borko *et al.*, (1992) followed the progress of students majoring in mathematics and science. One case study describes how a mathematics graduate failed to teach her class to divide fractions successfully. These researchers conclude that the failure had to do with the university teaching she had received. The topics taught were those oriented towards the research interests of the lecturers and not the Junior High School syllabus. The mathematics also involved a great deal of direct instruction in the use of computational techniques but did not treat the subject matter at higher levels of abstraction by encouraging the class to develop proofs for the various algorithms. Similar problems no doubt exist in British universities, particularly ones where the main subjects are taught in the undergraduate departments and the subject method in the faculty of education.

While in the education department, the mathematics student in Borko *et al.'s* (1992) case study still had problems. The 'methods' course emphasized 'conceptual' rather than 'procedural' knowledge, as defined in Table 5.1. The course, therefore, attempted to provide ideas which would give meaning to mathematical procedures. Teaching the division of fractions in this way would require the support of concrete and semi-concrete models, such as rods, drawings and other apparatus. The teacher would also need to put in scaffolding so that pupils could appreciate the links between different ideas. In this way pupils could not only learn to do the calculations but understand the procedures being used to obtain correct answers. However, at the end of the course the same mathematics graduate had gained little conceptual understanding. This was in part because the method tutor, due to the limited time available to cover all the topics, tended to work through demonstration rather than providing workshop experiences. The student came to see the tutor's 'scaffolding' as a set of routines similar to those experienced on her undergraduate course. For example, the method tutor often used paper folding or colouring in squares for illustration. The student, thinking these were routine procedures, used them automatically irrespective of the task demand. Neither was her limited understanding improved by her school experience. Although the school mentor claimed to believe in teaching for conceptual rather than procedural understanding, the student only ever saw her use direct instruction. This was because the need to produce high grades, as part of the district accountability programme, forced the teacher to concentrate on the procedures required for the test (Eisenhart *et al.*, 1993). These two factors – curriculum overload and the publication of 'league tables' – are, of course, also part of the contemporary primary education 'scene' in this country.

Even if all these problems could be overcome, it must be asked whether the efforts would be worth the gain. Better motivated and knowledgeable pupils would still be turned off science after a short time in the secondary schools. Few systematic studies of secondary school practice have been carried out since the early 1970s, but all the anecdotal evidence suggests things have changed little since then in those subjects with a hierarchical structure where note-taking, copying and colouring diagrams and writing up experiments still dominate the curriculum. A better choice may be to avoid the need to specialize at primary level and concentrate instead on improving motivation, providing basic skills (including the new basics such as information technology and citizenship) and developing a capacity to employ thinking 'for theory change'. This would allow policy makers to concentrate on improving subject expertise in the lower half of the secondary schools and in examining ways of allocating time more effectively. Possible structural change which dispensed with rigid year groups might, for example, end the usual arrangements where a teacher sees a large number of children from different classes for one or two periods each week. This sometimes makes it difficult to put faces to names, let alone establish the kinds of relationship which in Chapter 5 were deemed necessary for effective learning involving conceptual change. After all, if increased specialization and more class teaching play an essential part in raising standards in primary schools, why, under a similar system, are there so many reports of disaffected pupils at secondary level?

Induction and Professional Development

The above discussion, although veering on the polemical towards the end is, in part, a plea to redress the balance in INSET provision so that courses in what Shulman (1986) described as 'pedagogic knowledge of teaching' would be given greater prominence. Even if satisfactory programmes of initial training can be devised, they cannot of themselves (particularly with the government's plans to reduce the length of time for B.Ed. courses) produce the teacher with all the pedagogic skills required. Our present system, however, tends to operate as though this were the case. Initial teacher training, including the one-year PGCE programmes, are required to train students so that by the end of the course they have experience of all the major teaching strategies, having probably not had the time to concentrate on mastering any one effectively. But it is rare, for example, to come across an INSET course dealing with pedagogic questions such as classroom control unless it is for remediation. It is assumed that the basic requirements were mastered during initial training and 'honed' by experience during the first few years on the job.

This approach offers one reason why practice is so resistant to change, namely, there is *no* expectation that it should change. Student teachers model their methods on a more experienced classroom teacher's practice when acquiring these basic teaching skills. If they find themselves with problems, they may modify these procedures by taking advice from other teachers but, otherwise, with minor modifications, they stick with the system that works. There is then, in teaching, no accepted notion of a progression on which to base professional development. As they gain experience, teachers are not encouraged to

142

adopt new approaches for dealing with classroom discipline through negotiation or to handle relationships in ways that encourage pupils to be self-motivated. It is more often a case of having found one method that works and then sticking to it. This was true when, for example, Rogers offered courses on using less confrontational methods of control – what Gordon (1974) termed 'nobody wins' as opposed to 'teacher wins you lose' approaches. He was told by teachers 'you can't teach an old dog new tricks', to which he replied, 'But we are not dogs. We're people!' (Rogers, 1990, p.276).

Eisenhart *et al.* (1991) argue that there is no expectation of progression or development within pedagogy because 'there are no theories of how teachers learn to teach more effectively'. Both Kagan (1992) and Reynolds (1992) have reviewed the extensive literature on teaching and professional development and concur with Berliner's (1992) view that probably the best available model for building such a theory is one which seeks to differentiate between the cognitive states of teachers at different stages of their development. This is because appropriate training programmes can then be devised in the same way that different approaches are needed to move pupils to the point where they become independent thinkers. This notion of needing to match INSET training to the teacher's stage of professional development leads to a very different conclusion from Alexander (1992) when accounting for the failure of the Leeds Primary Needs Programme. This point will be taken up later in the chapter.

The model of expertise advanced by Berliner (1992) is based on studies of artificial intelligence. One area of interest has concerned the attempt to construct computer programmes which could outperform chess grand masters. These experts, for example, seem to retain in the memory a vast array of complicated positions which allows them to select an appropriate move without the need for the kind of elaborate evaluation required by the computer (Chase and Simon, 1973). Current computers, capable of carrying out 166 million calculations each second, have now finally triumphed. Interestingly, given the discussion in the previous chapter on motivation and self-esteem, the human expert put his loss down to 'a lack of concentration' because of 'fear of failure' at the thought of losing to a machine (*The Observer*, 4 September 1994, p.2).

According to Glasser and Chi (1988), experts across a variety of domains possess similar qualities. Expertise generally cannot be transferred from one domain to another. Chess grand masters are not usually gourmet chefs. More importantly, experts are distinguished from the experienced competent performer by their ability to recognize meaningful patterns quickly, irrespective of the particular context in which they operate. The experts' approach to problem-solving is therefore based on trying to understand the nature of the problem rather than applying a series of routines on a trial and error basis. Not surprisingly, therefore, experts are much quicker at problem-solving which is the reason why the grand masters can compete with the computer. By definition, true experts in any field will be limited in number.

Expertise appears to result from a combination of experience and specialist knowledge structures (Glasser and Chi, 1988). Clearly, not all experienced teachers become experts although they move considerably beyond the novice stage to a point where they begin to feel 'comfortable' and 'relaxed' in the classroom. Teachers in Nias' (1988) study estimated it took at least five years to reach this point.

The model of teaching expertise put forward by Berliner (1992) is based on a classification drawn up by Dreyfus and Dreyfus (1986). They posit the existence of five stages in the transition from novice to expert; they call these stages that of novice, advanced beginner, competent, proficient and expert. This classification has been used by Benner (1984) to study clinical nursing practice. The Dreyfus model is a situational rather than a trait one, because the skills or attributes required to progress from one stage to another can only be acquired by working in real situations and not through principles and theories learnt in the course of a programme of study.

Although there has been a considerable number of studies on differences between novices and experts, the definition of expert has often been problematic. In some cases, as Berliner (1992) observes, expertise has been equated solely with experience. In any model of professional development, therefore, more attention needs to be given to identifying expert teachers and studying the ways in which they differ from experienced competent colleagues. The model predicts that competent teachers, unlike novices and advanced beginners, have gained sufficient experience to be able to look ahead beyond the immediate situation and therefore to prioritize decisions about which task to tackle, which people to deal with, which behaviour to comment on and which to ignore. Thus, for the first time, the teacher begins to consider problems as they occur in a conscious analytical way. However, unlike experts, this problem-solving takes place within a context of very explicit pre-planning. Such an approach, therefore, tends to be inflexible and somewhat slower than the expert's because competent teachers refer each aspect of the situation to the plan. Gradually, as they become more proficient, competent teachers gain the ability to detect what Benner (1984, p.100) has termed the 'early warning signals' indicating a likely deterioration in the situation. Problem-solving speeds up and becomes more successful. However, and this is a crucial point, both competent and proficient teachers, unlike experts, operate in problem-solving situations by applying a set of principles or 'maxims' which serve as guidelines for their practice. The expert, on the other hand, operates with only one maxim, namely, that 'circumstances alter cases' because, as Berliner (1992) points out, the actions of expert teachers appear strongly influenced by a 'respect for their students'. Expert teachers are more concerned with understanding the reasons for pupils' behaviour than applying well-tried routines to eliminate or suppress it. The actions of the teacher (p.121) who dealt effectively with a classroom disturbance in which a boy pupil made a girl cry follows this pattern closely. Because of these attitudes, experts are more likely to use informal rather than 'bureaucratic' mechanisms to control their pupils and to prefer more indirect approaches (Berliner, 1992). This, in turn, demands a greater degree of improvisation with heavy reliance on exiting rather than entry strategies for maintaining the pace and the structure of the lesson.

Two examples may illustrate the way competent and proficient teachers use maxims to problem-solve and make decisions in the classroom. Galton (1989) has observed that in many situations teachers operate two-stage theories of teaching as a guide to practice. One such theory concerns the development of pupil's self-image and intrinsic motivation so that they are better prepared to work independently of the teacher in solving their own problems. As was noted in the previous chapter, because tasks which make more complex intellectual demands carry higher risks of failure, unconfident students with low self-esteem may adopt avoidance strategies in such situations and develop a dependency on teachers. The two-stage theory, most often used to deal with this problem, is guided discovery. Initially, the teacher gives considerable support and help so that the student can achieve a satisfactory outcome. On future occasions, when similar task demands are made, this help is gradually reduced as the student's confidence builds until a point in time where the pupil is prepared to carry out the task unaided. Stage one, therefore, involves considerable support, and stage two the withdrawal of that support.

This process was observed by Galton in a study of two teachers working with the same materials to teach a lesson with the same objectives using parallel classes (Galton and Williamson, 1992). As predicted by Berliner (1992) the teacher who had been identified as an outstanding practitioner (both by peers and by the pupils) adopted more indirect approaches and placed less emphasis on procedural knowledge, unlike her competent colleague. In one lesson the pupils had to use a variety of media (paint, clay, etching) to represent movement during an improvised dance routine. The competent practitioner planned the sequence of lessons so that pupils would first use one medium and then move on to another at a later point. During the initial lesson, considerable guidance was given in helping children to master the use of the particular medium they had chosen. By the end of the lesson, most children had produced a satisfactory outcome. When asked about her strategy, the teacher concerned replied,

> Just praise and encouragement and giving them help in problem solving activities until eventually they will become more skilled and they will not require me for things like that. It is all part of this growing independence.

The expert's approach was very different. All pupils were initially required to make a rough sketch. They then had to elaborate on this drawing, then experiment with the various media before deciding which one would be the most appropriate to represent their ideas. In contrast, the competent teacher decided which pupil would work in which medium. Thus by the end of the first lesson, few of the pupils in this second class had reached a situation where they had anything concrete to show for their efforts. Initially, the framework in which the children were allowed to operate was highly structured and tightly controlled. Pupils were told that they had to use a biro and not a pencil to make their rough sketches. It was explained that this was to stop them rubbing out and attempting to produce a perfect representation. The teacher said it was more important to 'get the feeling of movement from the eye to the hand and onto the paper'. At the same time, she also told the pupils that they could, if they wished, make these rough sketches on small pieces of paper rather than attempting to cover the whole sheet during their first attempts. When asked the reason for this decision, the teacher replied,

> I think there ought to be times for big choices for pupils but there are also occasions when I narrow it down deliberately so that they can focus their attention and not become worried about having to do such a large task.

Here the expert teacher intuitively recognizes the implications of Doyle's (1986) notion of task ambiguity and attempts to deal with it in an interesting way. Recognizing that covering a large piece of paper with their drawings without an opportunity to correct mistakes would make the pupils anxious, she deliberately reduces the risk by requiring them to make a small sketch in the corner of the paper. Later in the lesson she even dealt with the problem of children who were concerned about having too small a drawing by telling them that they could, with other members of the group, stick the various small drawings together to make a larger one if they wished.

It is clear that this teacher was much more interested in children exploring ways of representing motion before going on to produce a finished product. Her two-stage theory consisted of first, building up pupils' confidence in their ability to perform the task unaided by controlling the conditions under which they worked, and second, allowing them to perform a similar more demanding task but this time to control the conditions for themselves. She says of the lesson,

> At some point I was deliberately wanting to encourage them by suggesting they could do it a lot easier. That way I could have ended the lesson in five minutes, if I had told them. What is interesting to me is the stage they were actually at when it came down to them making their own decision. For me, it is so important to hear what they are saying and listen and watch how they are coping. I feel it is important that it is not just the task or the end product that I judge their work by.

Here then, children's motivation and self-confidence are developed by first reducing the risk of failure. In setting the task, the emphasis was on a question: 'How to do it?', unlike the strategy used by the competent teacher which gave greater importance to a statement: 'What to do'. Success in the expert's classroom was achieved with minimum teacher support. The confidence of the pupils was then boosted. At the second stage the task demands were greater, thereby increasing the risks but offering more satisfaction for successful achievement. This boosts self-image and develops a willingness to take more risks subsequently. In the competent teacher's case, pupils were free to work on difficult tasks from the beginning but with considerable teacher guidance. This strategy rested on the belief that satisfactory achievement of a product which looked 'authentic' would boost confidence and self-esteem. On subsequent occasions the pupils would then be willing to attempt equally difficult tasks without the same degree of teacher support.

An even more obvious example of a 'two-stage theory' concerns the key area of classroom management. Here the theory is more usually known as 'don't smile until Christmas'. At stage one, the class are firmly told, at the beginning of the school year, that they will operate under the strict rules and procedures devised by the teacher. Once pupils have 'internalized' these routines, so that their response to the teacher's requirements becomes automatic, stage two is introduced. The teacher now begins to relax and to allow an occasional joke during class. Activities requiring children to work independently of the teacher and to act responsibly are now introduced to vary the curriculum diet and make the teaching more interesting.

Often these more flexible 'stage two' arrangements incorporate a number of routine procedures which allow the teacher to cope with 'awkward' situations where it is anticipated problems could occur. Typical situations include pupils leaving the teacher's corner of the classroom, after a briefing, to continue working in their base or clearing their tables at the end of the session. Competent teachers have routines for moving pupils by turns from the mat to their place of work. Generally, the sequence begins with a recognized controlling measure; for example, the teacher will call for quiet and tell pupils to fold their arms. Then the group who are first to comply with these instructions are told to get up and go quietly to their places. At the end of the session, children may be told to clear and clean their tables, put up their chairs and stand quietly. Again, the first table to comply with these instructions is told to go out to play first.

When asked to explain these routine practices, teachers stress the importance of providing a clear structure based upon rules which are fair and that can be consistently operated. However, as Galton (1989) has observed, these rules are not always operated fairly or consistently. This can happen, for example, if on the occasions when the teacher detects, from one of Benner's (1984) early warning signals, that trouble may be brewing, the potential trouble-maker will be got out of the classroom as quickly as possible! Isolating this pupil from the rest of the class rather than making a fair selection according to the criterion of tidiness takes priority.

More importantly, the second reason why teachers are not consistently fair is that, as Gordon (1974) has observed, to work in this way requires teachers 'to deny their humanity' and to strive to be perfect. The expert teacher tends to accept this view and, therefore, appreciates that the notion of fairness is in itself problematic. What seems fair and reasonable to the teacher might not be looked at in the same way by the pupil. For example, Galton (1989) describes a lesson where a pupil called Michael accused the teacher of being unfair because, 'Ian talked a lot and you did nowt! I talked once and you did me!'. From the teacher's point of view, Michael had talked to Ian precisely at the moment when the class had quietened down. The fresh exchange had unsettled the rest of the class and given rise to another sequence of disruptions. Ian's previous interventions had occurred during the settling-in period. However, from Michael's point of view, the teacher's action appeared to be inconsistent and therefore unfair. In a class of 30 pupil this is always likely to be the case no matter how hard the teacher tries to operate the rules consistently. That is why expert teachers abandon the 'be fair and consistent' maxim and do occasionally smile before Christmas! Instead, they attempt to get pupils to engage in learning as 'theory change' by developing a new concept of fairness as 'inconsistency explained'. This involves teachers and pupils learning to appreciate each other's needs in the manner exemplified by the teacher in the previous chapter when dealing with the fight between a boy and a girl pupil.

Analysing behaviour management along a continuum in the manner above contrasts sharply with the present official procedure which concerns itself with the outcomes rather than the processes. For example, during an official inspection teachers must demonstrate that they can control a class effectively. The official OFSTED handbook informs the reader that behaviour and discipline in the classroom,

> are to be judged by the extent to which the attitude and actions of pupils contribute to or restrict effective learning in the classroom and the quality of life and functioning of the school as an orderly community. (OFSTED, 1992, p.7)

These judgements are to be based upon observation of standards of behaviour and the quality of relationships in the playground and in the classroom. The evidence used to determine the effectiveness of these practices includes frequency of exclusions and referrals, the existence of adequate codes of conduct, and rewards and sanctions for behaviour. Presumably, these criteria could be used to describe as effective those classrooms where teachers use what was referred to earlier (p.123) as 'dog training methods'. Routines are developed around games or rhymes such as,

Look at the window,
look at the door,
look at the ceiling,
look at the floor,
now look at me.

These procedures rely heavily on conditioning and might be expected to be used more frequently in novice teacher's classes where there is a greater likelihood of a breakdown in control. The model of professional development, when applied to behaviour management, might be described as a progression from these conditioning approaches, through the use of maxims such as 'firm but fair' until, as teachers grew more confident, 'humanistic' approaches based on the concept of fairness as 'inconsistency explained' were incorporated into the repertoire.

Observation of expert and competent teachers could identify similar progressions covering other competences to do with planning and monitoring, as well as the stages from extrinsic to intrinsic motivation described previously.

A major advantage of this approach to pedagogy is that it creates an expectation of change from the beginning until the end of a teacher's career. At the moment, provided that the methods used meet the Training Agency's or OFSTED's criteria of competence, there is little incentive for a teacher to become an expert practitioner. The model could be used in appraisal and in action planning to provide a 'mode of discourse' which was intellectually satisfying and avoided the use of catch-all phrases such as 'formal' or 'informal'. It would also be of value in the selection and training of mentors for school-focused initial teacher education. A novice is clearly much more likely to operate successfully when following the practice of a competent teacher who is not too far ahead along the stages of development, in much the same way as the zone of proximal development applies to children's cooperative learning. At present schools tend to choose the most experienced (and most expensive) teachers as mentors. To take a previous example, novices need to learn to use the competent teacher's routines for moving children in and out of the classroom before attempting to dismiss the class with a general instruction to, 'leave the room when your desks are clear'! Teachers with greater expertise would be asked to work with more experienced competent teachers in the same way that musical maestros offer 'master classes' to those who are already highly proficient performers. Since expertise is limited, the value of bringing these teachers together under one roof, in keeping with Hargreaves' (1990) suggestion for the establishment of teaching 'hospital schools', takes on an added attraction.

Training Methods and Teachers' Professional Development

Benner's (1984) analysis of clinical nurse training concluded that there were crucial links between the stage of development of the trainee and the appropriateness of a particular method of training. Because novices and beginners are more personally focused, that is, they judge requests to change practice by setting the effort required against the benefit it might bring them, Benner concludes that the most appropriate form of training is direct coaching. This method minimizes the expenditure of personal effort required of the learner. The task is defined for the trainee, then demonstrated by the trainer and practised by the trainee. If this practice is judged not to meet the required standard, the task is re-taught and further practice opportunities provided. Subsequent 'on the job' performance is monitored and 'fine-tuned' until the new procedures are being routinely used. Coaching of this kind clearly involves using many of the procedures developed for the direct instruction style of teaching: each task is broken down into small steps so that initial success is guaranteed and confidence is boosted.

As teachers enter the competent stage, and the ability to anticipate potential problems and to perceive overall patterns to events has begun to develop, Benner concluded that the best way to bring about further improvements in practice was through the use of a case study approach in which other teachers' practice is observed and analysed. This process involves a similar kind of reflection as that which McIntyre (1994) suggests operates, primarily at a technical level. The teacher makes 'deliberate use of ideas from a wide variety of sources' and also theorizes 'about these ideas in relation to a wide range of criteria including some at the practical and critical levels' (p.45). Improvements in practice have to be undertaken by providing theories or frameworks by which to conduct the analysis because, at this stage, teachers can only engage in problem-solving by means of 'maxims'.

It is only at the final stage, when proficient teachers are developing their skills to a high level, that 'reflection through action' becomes appropriate. This is because, by this stage, teachers are becoming more 'pupil-oriented' and tend to think of solutions to problems in terms of the pupils' needs as well as their own. Action research is therefore now the preferred training approach where the teacher's interpretation of events is checked against that of an outside consultant and sometimes the pupils. In the Leeds PNP programme, as far as one can judge, much of the school-based INSET activity involving primary needs coordinators made use of procedures incorporating this third level of reflection. Given the admission (Alexander 1991) that schools and teachers 'started from a very low base', it is likely that only a minority of teachers would have learned to operate this approach successfully. There seems to have been very little attempt on the part of the coordinators to engage in direct coaching. Instead, for reasons to do with power relationships within the school, they preferred to work alongside teachers and hope that their own practice would 'rub off' by some process of osmosis.

Some evidence in support of Benner's approach comes from the SCENE evaluation (Galton *et al.,* 1991) referred to earlier in Chapter 5. This project was concerned with enhancing the curriculum provision and practice of teachers in small rural schools. Although the programmes differed in each local authority, most employed advisory teachers and external coordinators to run the programmes of curriculum reform. In their analysis, the SCENE evaluation team developed a classification of professional development among the various clusters or groups of schools which fits very closely with Berliner's (1992) stage model of teacher development. For simplicity, the SCENE model consisted of three stages: initiation, consolidation and reorientation. Teachers at the initiation stage were very suspicious of the new curriculum development and wanted to examine the personal costs of involvement, very much as predicted by Doyle and Ponder's (1977) practicality ethic. Only when persuaded that there were positive gains in taking part (for example, although joint cluster planning took up additional free time it helped overcome feelings of isolation and boosted confidence), did these teachers become committed to the project and move to the second stage, that of consolidation.

Now the main focus was on translating the plans into action by developing suitable tasks. These teachers were keen to call in the subject advisers for help. When visiting each other's classes the discussion centred on the best way to present the task, ways of using resources and overcoming problems of implementation. At this stage the teachers were very similar to those described as competent in Berliner's model. Very little change in pedagogy was observed. Most of these teachers made use of this jointly developed curriculum but did so by 'bolting' these new tasks and procedures onto their existing practice. Only by the third stage, the reorientation stage, when the teachers no longer wanted external support but wished to take up the running of the programme for themselves, did the focus shift away from the content of the curriculum and begin to concentrate on the needs of pupils. Tasks and programmes as originally presented were now modified, because teachers perceived there to be better ways of doing things for themselves. The focus now began to shift to pedagogic concerns. However, during the lifetime of the SCENE project only a few clusters of teachers reached this reorientation stage.

It is clear from the evidence presented in previous chapters that even now primary teachers are nowhere near approaching this reorientation stage in their engagement with the National Curriculum. This is wholly predictable from theories of curriculum change discussed in Chapter 1. Top-down models of curriculum which are imposed on schools on the advice of experts cause teachers to look outside themselves for solutions to problems of implementation. When the experts' advice is 'fuzzy' or couched in generalities, the classroom teacher operates the 'practicality ethic' and does the minimum necessary to satisfy statutory requirements. When the experts' advice is largely generated from experience of secondary education and appears alien to the culture of primary schooling, indifference turns to resistance and dissatisfaction reaches crisis levels. This is what appears to have happened.

Personal Postscript: The Future 'Plowdenism'

In the final analysis, the crisis in the primary curriculum will not disappear simply by reducing the demands of the National Curriculum and providing a moratorium for teachers to master the various programmes of study and the revised assessment procedures. Curriculum building needs to start from the opposite direction, where relationships between learning and teaching are clearly articulated and the nature of knowledge required by various task demands, as these relate to how children think and learn, made explicit. The section on Plowdenism in Chapter 5 (p.98) began with a quotation which was written at a time when there was a general consensus about the need for an education system which provided similar opportunities for all children, irrespective of their background. Despite differences in rhetoric, it may be that the present consensus on pedagogy, both from the right and from the new 'radical' left, means that this objective is no longer considered feasible or desirable. Many of those in power, or who aspire to power, have themselves benefited enormously from the maintenance of the privileged status quo. It is to their advantage to push for a curriculum in which a great deal of subject matter is to be delivered through the medium of direct instruction because a majority of pupils will continue to display dependency and not to think for themselves. In this way they are less likely to challenge the existing system.

Sentiments of this kind are usually regarded by the media as overtly ideological. But a form of primary practice based on more than direct instruction, and a theory of learning to teach which gives all novices the expectation that they must work throughout their careers to improve their pedagogic skills, only makes sense if it is designed to promote the principles of justice and fairness which were enshrined in the original Plowden Report and which, as this century comes to a close, we are still struggling to realize.

References

Abbott, D. with Broadfoot, P., Croll, P., Osborn, M. and Pollard, A. (1994) 'Some sink, some float: Curriculum assessment and accountability', *British Educational Research Journal*, 20, 2, 155–74.

ACT (1992) 'Educational planning and assessment system', *Content Validity of ACT's Education Achievement Tests*, Fowa: American College Testing Programme.

Alexander, P., Schallert, D. and Hare, V. (1991) 'Coming to terms: How researchers in learning and literacy talk about knowledge', *Review of Educational Research*, 61, 3, 315–43.

Alexander, R. (1984) *Primary Teaching*, London: Holt, Reinhart and Winston.

Alexander, R. (1988) 'Garden or jungle: Teachers development and informal primary education' in Blyth, W. (ed.) *Informal Primary Education Today: Essays and Studies*, London: Falmer Press.

Alexander, R. (1991) *Primary Education in Leeds*, Twelfth and Final Report from the Primary Needs Independent Evaluation Project: University of Leeds.

Alexander, R. (1992) *Policy and Practice in Primary Education*, London: Routledge.

Alexander, R. (1993) 'Innocence and Experience: Reconstructing Primary Education', Inaugural Lecture given at the University of Leeds, 13 December.

Alexander, R., Rose, J. and Woodhead, C. (1992) *Curriculum Organisation and Classroom Practice in Primary Schools*, London: Department of Education and Science.

Alexander, R., Willcocks, J. and Kinder, K. (1989) *Changing Primary Practice*, London: Falmer Press.

Anthony, W. S. (1982) 'Research on progressive teaching', *British Journal of Educational Psychology*, 52, 381–5.

Apple, M. (1982) *Education and Power*, London: Routledge & Kegan Paul.

APU (1989) *Science at Age 13: Review of APU Survey Findings*, London: HMSO.

Ashton, P., Henderson, E. and Peacock, A. (1989) *Teacher Education Through Classroom Evaluation: The principles and practice of IT-INSET*, London: Routledge.

Auld, R. (1976) *The William Tyndale Junior and Infants Schools*, A report of the public inquiry, London: ILEA.

Ball, S. (1981) *Beachside Comprehensive*, London: Cambridge University Press.

Ball, S. (1990) *Policies and Policy Making in Education*, London: Routledge.

Bandura, A. (1986) *Social Foundations of Thought and Action*, Englewood Cliffs NJ: Prentice Hall.

Barrett, G. (1986) *Starting School: An Evaluation of the Experience*, Final Report to the AMMA, CARE, University of East Anglia.

Benner, P. (1984) *From Novice to Expert: Excellence and power in clinical nursing practice*. Reading, Mass: Addison-Wesley.

Bennett, N. (1976) *Teaching Styles and Pupil Progress*, London: Open Books.

Bennett, N. (1992) *Managing Learning in the Primary School*, Association for the Study of Primary Education, Chester: Trentham Books.

154

Bennett, N. and Carré, C. (eds) (1993) *Learning to Teach*, London: Routledge.

Bennett, N. and Dunne, E. (1992) *Managing Classroom Groups*, Hemel Hampstead: Simon and Schuster.

Bennett, N., Wragg, E., Carré, C. and Carter, D. (1992) 'A longitudinal study of primary teachers perceived competence in and concerns about National Curriculum implementation', *Research Papers in Education*, 7, 53–78.

Benton, P. (1990) (ed.) *The Oxford Internship Scheme: Intergration and partnership in initial teacher training*, London: Calouste Gulbenkian Foundation.

Berliner, D. (1992) 'Some characteristics in experts in the pedagogical domain', in Oser, F., Dick, A. and Patry, J. (eds) *Effective and Responsible Teaching: The New Synthesis*, San Francisco, CA: Jossey-Bass.

Borko, H. and Livingston, C. (1989) 'Cognition and Improvisation: Differences in mathematics instruction by expert and novice teachers', *American Educational Research Journal*, 26, 4, 473–98.

Borko, H., Eisenhart, M., Brown, C., Underhill, R., Jones, D. and Agard, P. (1992) 'Learning to teach hard mathematics', *Journal of Research in Mathematics Education*, 23, 3, 194–222.

Bowles, S. and Gintis, H. (1976) *Schooling in Capitalist America*, London: Routledge & Kegan Paul.

Brophy, J. E. and Good, T. L. (1986) 'Teacher behaviour and student achievement', in Wittrock, M. C. (ed.) *Handbook of Research on Teaching*, 3rd ed, New York: Macmillan.

Brown, A. and Palincsar, A. (1986) *Guided Cooperative Learning and Individual Knowledge Acquisition*, Technical Report 372, Cambridge, Mass: Bolt, Beranak and Newham Inc.

Bruner, J. (1985) 'Vygotsky: A historical and conceptual perspective', in Wertsch, J. (ed.) *Culture, Communication and Cognition*, Cambridge: Cambridge University Press.

Burstall, C. and Kay, B. (1978) *Assessment: The American Experience*, London: Department of Education and Science.

Calderhead, J. (1987) 'The quality of reflection in student teachers professional learning', *European Journal of Teacher Education*, 10, 3, 269–78.

Callaghan, J. (1976) 'Towards a National Debate – The Prime Minister's Ruskin speech', *Education*, 22 October, 332–3.

Callaghan, J. (1992) 'The Education Debate I', in William, M. Dougherty, R. and Banks, F. (eds) *Continuing the Education Debate*, London: Cassell.

Campbell, J. (1985) *Developing the Primary School Curriculum*, London: Holt, Rinehart and Winston.

Campbell, R. (1993) 'A dream at conception: a nightmare at delivery', in Campbell, R. (ed.) *Breadth and Balance in the Primary Curriculum*, London: Falmer Press.

Campbell, R. and Neill, S. (1990) *1130 Days*, First report on research into the use of teacher time, London: Assistant Masters and Mistresses Association (AMMA).

Campbell, R. and Neill, S. (1991) *Workloads, Achievement and Stress*, Second report on research into the use of teacher time, London: Assistant Masters and Mistresses Association (AMMA).

Campbell, R. and Neill, S. (1992) *Teacher Time and Curriculum Manageability at Key Stage 1*, Third report on research into the use of teacher time, London: Assistant Masters and Mistresses Association (AMMA).

Carter, K., Cushing, K., Sabers, D., Stein, D. and Berliner, D. (1988) 'Expert-novice differences in perceiving and processing visual classroom information', *Journal of Teacher Education*, 39, 3, 25–31.

Cato, V. and Whetton, C. (1990) *Enquiry into LEA Evidence on Standards of Reading of Seven Year Old Children,* Slough: NFER.

Cavendish, S., Galton, M., Hargreaves, L. and Harlen, W. (1990) *Assessing Science in the Primary Classroom: Observing Activities,* London: Paul Chapman.

CDCC (1982) (Council for Cultural Cooperation) *Primary Education in Western Europe: Aims, problems, trends,* Report of a Council of Europe Project No 8 Seminar held at Vaduz, Liechtenstein, Strasbourg: Council of Europe (DECS/EGT [83] 647).

CDCC (1987) (Council for Cultural Cooperation) *Development in Practice,* A Report on Education Centres as a Means of Introducing Innovation in Primary Education by Strittmatter, A. (Switzerland), Strasbourg: Council of Europe (DECS/EGT [87] 18).

CEB (1993) (Commissie Evaluatie Basisonderwys) *Primary Education in the Netherlands. Contexts, curricula, processes and results,* Final Evaluation Conference: Noordwijk, Netherlands.

Chase, W. and Simon, H. (1973) 'Perception in chess', *Cognitive Psychology*, 4, 55–81.

Clark, M. and Davies, D. (1981) 'Radical education: The pedagogical subtext', in Lawn, M. and Barton, L. (eds) *Rethinking Curriculum Studies,* Beckenham: Croom Helm.

Cooper, B. (1992) 'Testing National Curriculum mathematics: Some critical comments on the treatment of contexts for mathematics', *The Curriculum Journal*, 3, 3, 231–44.

Cortazzi, M. (1991) *Primary Teaching. How it is: A narrative account,* London: David Fulton Publishers.

Cowie, H., Smith, P., Boulton, M. and Laver, R. (1994) *Cooperation in the Mult-ethnic Classroom,* London: David Fulton Publishers.

Croll, P. and Moses, D. (1985) *One in Five: The assessment and incidence of special educational needs,* London: Routledge & Kegan Paul.

Dainton Report (1968) *Enquiry into the Flow of Candidates in Science and Technology into Higher Education,* Cmnd 3541, London: HMSO.

Dearing, R. (1993a) *The National Curriculum and its Assessment: An Interim Report,* York: National Curriculum Council and Schools Examination and Assessment Council.

Dearing, R. (1993b) *The National Curriculum and its Assessment: Final Report,* London: Schools Curriculum and Assessment Authority.

Deci, E. and Chandler, C. (1986) 'The importance of motivation for the failure of the L.D. field', *Journal of Learning Disability*, 19, 10, 587–94.

Deci, E. and Ryan, R. (1985) *Intrinsic Motivation and Self Determination in Human Behaviour,* New York: Plenum Press.

Delamont, S. and Galton, M. (1984) *Inside the Secondary School,* London: Routledge & Kegan Paul.

Denham, C. and Liberman, A. (eds) (1980) *Time to Learn,* Report of the beginning teacher education studies, Washington DC: National Institute of Education.

DES (1980) *A Framework for the School Curriculum,* London: HMSO.

DES (1983) *Curriculum 11-16: Towards a Statement of Entitlement: Curricular reappraisal in action,* London: HMSO.

DES (1985a) *The Curriculum from 5–16,* London: HMSO.

DES (1985b) *Better Schools,* Cmnd 9469, London: HMSO.

156

DfE (1994) *Assessing 7 and 11 year olds in 1995*, Cirçular 21/94, London: Department for Education.

Desforges, C. Holden, C. and Hughes, M. (1994) 'Assessment at Key Stage One: Its effects on parents, teachers and classroom practice', *Research Papers in Education*, 9, 2, 133–58.

Doyle, W. (1986) 'Classroom organisation and management' in Wittrock, M. (ed.) *Third Handbook of Research on Teaching*, New York: Macmillan, 392–431.

Doyle, W and Ponder, G (1977) 'The practicality ethic and teacher decision making', *Interchange*, 8, 1–12.

Dreyfus, H. and Dreyfus, S. (1986) *Mind Over Machine*, New York: Free Press.

Drummond, M. (1993) *Assessing Children's Learning*, London: David Fulton Publishers.

Edwards, T. (1994) 'The Universities Council for Education of Teachers: Defending an interest or fighting a course?', *Journal of Education for Teaching*, 20, 2, 143–52.

Eggleston, J., Galton, M. and Jones, M. (1976) *Processes and Products of Science Teaching*, Schools Council Research Series, Basingstoke: Macmillan Education.

Eisenhart, L., Behm, L. and Romagnano, L. (1991) 'Learning to teach: Developing expertise or rite of passage?', *Journal of Education for Teaching*, 17 1, 51–71.

Eisenhart, M., Borko, H., Underhill, R., Brown, C., Jones, D. and Agard, P. (1993) 'Conceptual knowledge falls through the cracks: Complexities of learning to teach mathematics for understanding', *Journal for Research in Mathematics Education*, 24, 4, 8–40.

Eraut, M. (1994) *Developing Professional Knowledge and Competence*, London: Falmer Press.

Everton, T. and Impey, G. (eds) (1989) *IT-INSET: Partnership in training, The Leicester experience*, London: David Fulton Publishers.

Featherstone, J. (1971) *Schools Where Children Learn*, New York: Liveright.

Flanders, N. A. (1964) 'Some relationships among teacher influence, pupil attitudes and achievement', in Biddle, B. J. and Ellena, W. J. (eds) *Contemporary Research on Teacher Effectiveness*, New York: Holt, Rinehart and Winston.

Fullan, M. (1992) *'What's Worth Fighting for in Headship'*, Buckingham: Open University Press.

Fullan, M. and Hargreaves, A. (1992) *What's Worth Fighting For in Your School*, Buckingham: Open University Press.

Furlong, V. Hirst, P. Pocklington, K. and Miles, S. (1988) *Initial Teacher Training and the Role of the School*, Buckingham: Open University Press.

Gage, N. L. (1985) *Hard Gains in the Soft Sciences: The Case of Pedagogy*, A CEDR Monograph. Indiana: Phi Delta Kappa.

Galton, M. (1981) 'Teaching groups in the junior school, a neglected art', *School Organisation*, 1, 2, 175–81.

Galton, M. (1987) 'An ORACLE chronicle: a decade of classroom research', *Teaching and Teacher Education*, 3, 4, 299–314.

Galton, M. (1989) *Teaching in the Primary School*, London: David Fulton Publishers.

Galton, M. and Blyth, A. (eds) (1989) *Handbook of Primary Education in Europe*, London: David Fulton Publishers for the Council of Europe.

Galton, M. and Croll, P. (1980) 'Pupil progress in basic skills', in Galton, M. and Simon, B. (eds) *Progress and Performance in the Primary Classroom*, London: Routledge & Kegan Paul.

Galton, M. and Patrick, H. (1990) *Curriculum Provision in the Small Primary School*,

London: Routledge.

Galton, M. and Simon, B. (eds) (1980) *Progress and Performance in the Primary Classroom*, London: Routledge & Kegan Paul.

Galton, M. and Willcocks, J. (1983) *Moving from the Primary Classroom*, London: Routledge & Kegan Paul.

Galton, M. and Williamson, J. (1992) *Group Work in the Primary Classroom*, London: Routledge.

Galton, M., Simon, B. and Croll, P. (1980) *Inside the Primary Classroom*, London: Routledge & Kegan Paul.

Galton, M., Fogelman, K., Hargreaves, L. and Cavendish, S. (1991) *The Rural Schools Curriculum Enhancement National Evaluation (SCENE) Project: Final Report*, London: Department of Education and Science.

Gardner, H. (1983) *Frames of Mind: The Theory of Multiple Intelligences*, New York: Basic Books.

Gipps, C. (1992) 'Equal opportunities and the Standard Assessment Tasks for 7 year olds', *The Curriculum Journal*, 3, 2, 171–84.

Gipps, C. and Goldstein, H. (1983) *Monitoring Children*, Oxford: Heinmann Educational.

Gipps, D., McCallum, B., McAlister, S. and Brown M. (1991) 'National Assessment at Seven: Some Emerging Themes', paper presented to the 1991 Conference of the British Educational Research Association.

Glasser, R. and Chi, M. (1988) 'The nature of expertise: An overview', in Chi, M. *et al.*, (eds) *The Nature of Expertise*, New York: Lawrence Erlbaum.

Golby, M. (1994) 'After Dearing: A critical review of the Dearing Report', *The Curriculum Journal*, 5, 1, 95–105.

Goldstein, H. (1986) 'Models for equating test scores and for studying comparability of public examinations' in Nuttall, D. (ed.), *Assessing Educational Achievement*, London: Falmer Press.

Goldstein, H. (1993) 'Improving assessment: A response to the BERA Policy Task Group's report on assessment', *The Curriculum Journal*, 4, 1, 121–3.

Goodlad, S. and Hurst, B. (1989) *Peer Tutoring: A Guide to Learning by Teaching*, London: Kogan Page.

Gordon, T. (1974) *TET: Teacher Effectiveness Training*, New York: Peter Wyden.

Gorwood, B. (1994) 'Primary-secondary transfer after the National Curriculum', in Pollard, A. and Bourne, J. (eds) *Teaching and Learning in the Primary School*, London: Routledge for the Open University.

Graham, D. with Tyler, D. (1993) *A Lesson For Us All: The Making of the National Curriculum*, London: Routledge.

Gray, J. (1979) 'Reading progress in English infant schools: Some problems emerging from a study of teacher effectiveness', *British Educational Research Journal*, 5, 2.

Gray, J. and Satterley, D. (1976) 'A chapter of errors: Teaching styles and pupil progress in retrospect', *Educational Research*, 19, 1, 45–56.

Grossman, P. (1992) 'Why models matter: An alternative view on professional growth in teaching', *Review of Educational Research*, 62, 2, 171–80.

Hadow Report (1931) *Report of the Consultative Committee on the Primary School*, London: HMSO.

Hammersley, M. and Scarth, J. (1993) 'Beware of wise men bearing gifts: A case study in the issue of educational research', *British Educational Research Journal*, 19, 5, 489–98.

Hargreaves, A. (1980) 'The ideology of the middle school', in Hargreaves, A. and Tickle, L. (eds) *Middle Schools: Origins, Ideology and Practice,* London: Harper and Row.

Hargreaves, D. (1990) *The Future of Teacher Education,* London: Hockerill Educational Foundation.

Harlen, W. (1983) *Guides to Assessment in Education: Science,* Basingstoke: Macmillan.

Harlen, W., Gipps, C., Broadfoot, D. and Nuttall, D. (1992) 'Assessment and the improvement of education', *The Curriculum Journal,* 3, 3, 215–30.

Hart, S. (1992) 'Differentiation, part of a problem or part of a solution', *The Curriculum Journal,* 3, 2, 131–42.

Hillgate Group (1989) *Learning to Teach,* London: Claridge Press.

Hilsum, S. and Cane, B. (1971) *The Teacher's Day,* Slough: NFER.

HMI (1978) *Primary Education in England: A Survey by HM Inspectors of Schools,* London, HMSO.

HMI (1982) *The New Teacher in School: A Report by Her Majesty's Inspectors,* Department of Education and Science. (Matters for Discussion, 15), London: HMSO

HMI (1983) *9–13 Middle Schools: An Illustrative Survey,* London: HMSO.

HMI (1987) *Quality in Schools: The Initial Training of Teachers,* London: HMSO.

Hunter, J., Turner, I., Russell, C., Trew, K. and Curry, C. (1993) 'Mathematics and the real world', *British Educational Research Journal,* 19, 1, 17–26.

James, M. and Conner, C. (1993) 'Are reliability and validity achievable in National Curriculum assessment? Some observations in moderation at Key Stage 1 in 1992', *The Curriculum Journal,* 4, 1, 5–20.

Johnson, S. and Bell, J. (1985) 'Evaluating and predicting survey efficiency using generalisability theory', *Journal of Educational Measurement,* 22, 2, 107–19.

Jones, D. (1987) 'Planning for Progressivism: The changing primary school in the Leicestershire Authority during the Mason Era 1947–71', in Lowe, R. (ed.) *The Changing Primary School,* London: Falmer Press.

Jones, D. (1988) *Steward Mason: The Art of Education,* London: Lawrence & Wishart.

Joyce, B. and Showers, B. (1983) 'Transfer of training: The contribution of coaching', *Journal of Education,* 163, 2, 163–72.

Kagan, D. (1992) 'Professional growth among preservice and beginning teachers', *Review of Educational Research,* 62, 2, 129–70.

Kliebard, H. (1986) *The Struggle for the American Curriculum 1893–1958,* New York: Methuen.

Kounin, J. (1970) *Discipline and Group Management in Classrooms,* New York: Holt, Rinehart and Winston.

Kyriacou, C. (1986) *Effective Teaching in Schools,* Oxford: Basil Blackwell.

Lawlor, S. (1988) *The Correct Core,* London: Centre for Policy Studies.

Lawlor, S. (1990) *Teachers Mistaught: Training in Theories or Education in Subjects,* Policy Study No 116, London: Centre for Policy Studies.

Lawn, M. and Barton, L. (eds) (1981) *Rethinking Curriculum Studies,* London: Croom Helm.

Lawton, D. (1975) *Class, Culture and the Curriculum,* London: Routledge and Kegan Paul.

Linn, R., Baker, E. and Dunbar, S. (1991) 'Complex performance-based assessment: Expectations and validation criteria', *Educational Researcher,* 20, 8, 15–21.

Lucas, P. (1991) 'Reflection, new practices, and the need for flexibility in supervising student teachers', *Journal of Further and Higher Education*, 15, 2, 84–93.

McIntyre, D. (1992) 'Theory, theorising and reflection in initial teacher education', in Calderhead, J. and Gates, P. (eds) *Conceptualising Reflection in Teacher Education*, London: Falmer Press.

McNamara, D. (1994) *Classroom Pedagogy and Primary Practice*, London: Routledge.

Meadows, S. (1993) *The Child as Thinker: The Development and Acquisition of Cognition in Childhood*, London: Routledge.

Measor, L. and Woods, P. (1984) *Changing Schools: Pupils' perspectives on transfer to a comprehensive*, Buckingham: Open University Press.

Messick, S. (1989) 'Validity' in Linn, R. (ed.) *Educational measurement*, 3rd edn, New York: Macmillan.

Messick, S. (1994) 'The interplay of evidence and consequences in the validation of performance assessments', *Educational Researcher*, 23, 2, 13–23.

Mortimore, P. and Mortimore, J. (eds) (1991) *The Primary Head: Roles, Responsibilities and Reflections*, London: Paul Chapman.

Mortimore, P., Sammons, P., Stoll, L. D. and Ecob, R. (1988) *School Matters: The Junior Years*, Wells: Open Books.

Moser, C. (1990) 'Our Need for an Informal Society', Presidential Address to the British Association, London.

NCC (1989) *A Framework for the Primary Curriculum, Guidance 1*, York: National Curriculum Council.

NCC (1993) *The National Curriculum at Key Stages 1 and 2: Advice to the Secretary of State for Education*, York: National Curriculum Council.

Newsom, J. (1963) *Half Our Future: A Report of the Central Advisory Council for Education (England)*, Chairman J. H. Newsom, London: HMSO.

Nias, J. (1988) 'Informal education in action: Teachers' accounts', in Blyth, A. (ed.) *Informal Primary Education Today*, London: Falmer Press.

Nias, J., Southworth, G. and Yeomans, R. (1989) *Staff Relationships in the Primary School*, London: Cassell.

O'Hear, A. (1988) *Who Teaches the Teachers*, London: Social Affairs Unit.

OFSTED (1922) *Handbook of Inspection of Schools*, London: Office for Standards in Education.

OFSTED (1993a) *Curriculum Organisation and Classroom Practice in Primary Schools: A follow up report*, London: Office for Standards in Education.

OFSTED (1993b) *National Curriculum: Possible ways forward*, London: Office for Standards in Education.

Patterson, J. Purkey, S. and Parker, J. (1986) *Productive School System for a Non-rational World*, Alexandria, VA: Associates for Supervision and Curriculum Development.

Pintrich, P., Marx, R. and Boyle, R. (1993) 'Beyond cold conceptual change: The role of motivational beliefs and classroom contextual factors in the process of conceptual change', *Review of Educational Research*, 63, 2, 167–200.

Plowden Report (1967) *Children and their Primary Schools, Report of the Central Advisory Council for Education in England*, London: HMSO.

Pollard, A. (1985) *The Social Word of the Primary School*, London: Holt, Rinehart and Winston.

Pollard, A. with Osborn, M., Abbott, D., Broadfoot, P. and Croll, P. (1993) 'Balancing priorities: Children and the curriculum in the nineties', in Campbell, R. (ed.) *Breadth and Balance in the Primary Curriculum*, London: Falmer Press.

160

Pring, R. (1989) *The New Curriculum*, London: Cassell.

Rasch, G. (1966) 'An item analysis which takes individual differences into account', *British Journal of Mathematical and Statistical Psychology*, 19, 1,49–57.

Resnick, A. and Collins, A. (1994) 'Cognition and learning', in Husén, T. and Postlethwaite, T. (eds) *The International Encyclopedia of Education*, Vol 2, 2nd ed, Oxford: Pergamon.

Reynolds, A. (1992) 'What is competent beginning teaching? A review of the literature', *Review of Educational Research*, 62, 1, 1–36.

Reynolds, J. and Skilbeck, M. (1976) *Culture and the Classroom*, London: Open Books.

Richards, C. (1982) 'Primary education 1974–80', in Richards, C. (ed.) *New Directions in Primary Education*, London: Falmer Press.

Rogers, B. (1990) *You Know the Fair Rule: Strategies for making the hard job of discipline in school easier*, Hawthorne, Victoria: ACER (Australian Council for Educational Research).

Rosenshine, B. (1979) 'Content, time and direct instruction', in Peterson, P. and Walberg, H. (eds) *Research on Teaching Concepts, Findings and Implications*, Berkeley, CA: McCutchan.

Rosenshine, B. (1987) 'Direct instruction', in Dunkin, M. (ed.) *Teaching and Teacher Education*, Oxford: Pergamon.

Rosenshine, B. and Furst, N. (1973) 'The use of direct observation to study teaching', in Travers, R. (ed.) *Second Handbook of Research on Teaching*, Chicago, IL: Rand McNally.

Rowe, B. (1985) 'Wait-time and rewards as instructional variables, their influence on language, logic and fate control', *Journal of Research in Science Teaching*, 11, 81–94.

Sammons, P., Lewis, A. MacLure, M., Riley, J. Bennett, N. and Pollard, A. (1994) 'Teaching and learning processes', in Pollard, A. (ed.) *Look Before You Leap, Research Evidence for the Curriculum at Key Stage 2*, London: Tufness Press.

Scarth, J. and Hammersley, M. (1986) 'Questioning ORACLE: An assessment of ORACLE's analysis of teachers' questions', *Educational Research*, 28, 3, 174–84.

Scarth, J. and Hammersley, M. (1987) 'More questioning of ORACLE: A reply to Croll and Galton', *Educational Research*, 29, 1, 37–46.

Schon, D. (1983) *The Reflective Practioner*, London: Temple Smith.

Schools Council (1983) *Primary Practice: A Sequel to 'The Practical Curriculum'*, Working Paper 75, London: Methuen.

SEAC (1991) *Pilot Study of Standard Assessment Tasks for Key Stage 1: A Report by the STAR Consortium*, London: Schools Examination and Assessment Council.

Sharp, R. and Green, A. (1975) *Education and Social Control: A Study in Progressive Primary Education*, London: Routledge & Kegan Paul.

Shorrocks, D., Daniels, S., Frobisher, L., Nelson, N. and Waterson, A. (1992) *Evaluation of National Curriculum Assessment at Key Stage 1*, London: Schools Examination and Assessment Council.

Shulman, L. (1986) 'Those who understand: Knowledge growth in Teaching', *Educational Research*, 15, 4–14.

Shulman, L. (1987) 'Knowledge and teaching: Foundations of the new reform', *Harvard Educational Review*, 57, 1, 1–22.

Simon, B. (1981a) 'Why no pedagogy in England?', in Simon, B. and Taylor, W. (eds) *Education in the Eighties, The Central Issues*, 124–45, London: Batsford.

Simon, B. (1981b) 'The primary school revolution: Myth or Reality?', in Simon, B. and

Willcocks, J. (eds) *Research and Practice in the Primary Classroom*, London: Routledge & Kegan Paul.

Simon, B. (1990) 'The Future of Education: Which way?', School of Education, University of Newcastle Upon Tyne Centenary Lecture.

Simon, B. (1993) 'Primary education', *Education Today and Tomorrow*, 44, 3, 13–14.

Simon, B. and Willcocks, J. (eds) (1981) *Research and Practice in the Primary Classroom*, London: Routledge & Kegan Paul.

Skilbeck, M. (1982) 'Three educational ideologies', in Martin, T. and Raggatt, P. (eds) *Challenge and Change in the Curriculum*, London: Hodder and Stoughton for the Open University.

Slavin, R. (1986) 'Small group methods', in Dunkin, M. (ed.) *The International Encyclopedia of Teaching and Teacher Education*, Oxford: Pergamon.

Stake, R. E. (1967) 'The countenance of educational evaluation', *Teachers College Record*, 68, 523–40.

Sternberg, R. (1990) 'T and T is an explosive combination: Technology and testing', *Educational Psychologist*, 25, 201–22.

Summers, M. (1994) 'Science in the primary school: The problem of teachers' curricular expertise', *The Curriculum Journal*, 5, 2, 179–94.

Summers, M., Kleiger, C. and Palacio, D. (1993) *Long Term Impact of a New Approach to Teacher Education for Primary Science, Project Report*, Oxford: Department of Educational Studies, University of Oxford.

TGAT (1988) *National Curriculum Task Group on Assessment and Testing*, chaired by Professor Paul Black, London: Department of Education and Science.

Thomas, N. (1993) 'Breadth, balance and the National Curriculum', in Campbell, R. (ed.) *Breadth and Balance in the Primary Curriculum*, London: Falmer Press.

Tizard, B., Blatchford, D., Burke, J., Farquhar. C. and Plewis, I. (1988) *Young Children at School in the Inner City*, Hove: Lawrence Erlbaum.

Tobin, K. (1983) 'Management of time in classrooms' in Fraser, B. (ed.) *Classroom Management*, Education Research and Workshop Mineograph No 1, Perth: Western Australian Institute of Technology.

Tomlinson, J. (1992) 'Retrospect on Ruskin: Prospect on the 1990s', in Williams, M. Dougherty, R. and Banks, F. (eds) *Continuing the Education Debate*, London: Cassell.

Torrance, H. (1991) 'Evaluating SATs', *Cambridge Journal of Education*, 21, 2, 129–40.

Van Den Brink, G. and Van Bruggen, J. (1990) 'Dutch curriculum response in the 1980s', *The Curriculum Journal*, 1, 3, 275–89.

Vanderberghe, R. (1984) 'Teachers' role in educational change', *British Journal of In-Service Education*, 11, 1, 14–25.

Warham, S. (1993) *Primary Teaching and the Negotiation of Powers*, London: Paul Chapman.

Warwick, D. (1987) *The Modular Curriculum*, Oxford: Basil Blackwell.

Watkins, P. (1993) Book review: 'A lesson for us all', *Headlines*, Journal of SHA, 11, 65–6.

Webb, N. (1989) 'Peer interaction and learning in small groups', *International Journal of Educational Research*, 13, 21–39.

Webb, R. (1993) *Eating the Elephant Bit by Bit: The National Curriculum at Key Stage 2*, final report of research commissioned by the Association of Teachers and Lecturers (ATL), London: ATL Publishers.

162

Weiner, B. (1986) *Attribution Theory of Motivation and Emotion,* New York: Springer-Verlag.

Wheeler, D. (1967) *Curriculum Process,* London: University of London Press.

Willcocks, B. and Eustace, P. (1980) *Tooling up for Curriculum Review,* Windsor: NFER.

Williams, R. (1961) *Culture and Society,* Harmondsworth: Penguin.

Willis, P. (1977) *Learning to Labour: How working class kids get working class jobs,* Farnborough: Saxon Houge.

Wood, D. (1988) *How Children Think and Learn,* Oxford: Basil Blackwell.

Wragg, E., Bennett, N. and Carré, C. (1989) 'Primary teachers and the National Curriculum', *Research Papers in Education,* 4, 12–37.

Young, M. (1971) *Knowledge and Control,* London: Collier-Macmillan.

Index

164